Winner's!
ENGLISH

Basic Lessons For Ukrainian Speakers

BOOKS 1 & 2
Lessons 1 - 40

Winner's! ENGLISH
Basic Lessons

Winner's! English Books

Copyright © 2022
All rights reserved.
ISBN: 9798445018643

These lessons are part of the series:

"Winner's! English – Basic Lessons For Ukrainian Speakers"
Book 1 (Lessons 1 – 20) +
Book 2 (Lessons 21 – 40)

CONTENTS

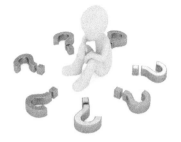

Numbers числа

one	two	three	four	five
1	2	3	4	5

six	seven	eight	nine	ten
6	7	8	9	10

eleven	twelve	thirteen	fourteen	fifteen
11	12	13	14	15

sixteen	seventeen	eighteen	nineteen	twenty
16	17	18	19	20

Days of the week Дні тижня

Monday, Tuesday, Wednesday, Thursday, Friday, Saturday, Sunday

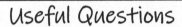

Useful Questions

How do you spell it? Як це пишеться?

What does this mean? Що це означає слово?

How do you say it in English? Як ви говорите по-англійськи?

This book belongs to:

_____

Lesson 1 — My pencil case

мій пенал

Part 1A: Learn the words

1. **a pencil**
   олівець
2. **an eraser**
   гумка
3. **some glue**
   клей
4. **a pencil sharpener**
   точилка
5. **some whiteout**
   коректор

6. **a pen**
   ручка
7. **a ruler**
   лінійка
8. **some tape**
   сантиметр
9. **a marker**
   маркер
10. **a crayon**
    кольоровий олівець

 Practice speaking: "олівець" is "<u>pencil</u>" in English!

Part 1B: Write the words

Write the missing letters!   Write x 1   Write x 2

1. __e__c__l   pencil _____   _____
2. p__n   _____   _____
3. __l__e   _____   _____
4. r__l__r   _____   _____
5. __e__c__l __h__rp__ner _____   _____
6. __r__s__r   _____   _____
7. w__i__e__u__   _____   _____
8. __a__e   _____   _____
9. m__r__e__   _____   _____
10. __r__y__n   _____   _____

Part 2A: Ask a question

What is <u>this</u>?

✓ **This is <u>a pencil</u>. It is not <u>a pen</u>.**

What is <u>that</u>?

✓ **That is <u>a crayon</u>. It isn't <u>a marker</u>.**

 **Winner's Tip!** isn't = is not

Part 2B: Fill in the blanks

1. what is _____?
   This _____ a ruler. _____ isn't _____.

2. _____ is that?
   _____ is _____. It isn't _____.

3. _____ is _____?
   That _____ some glue. It _____ _____.

4. _____ is _____?
   This is _____. _____ _____ some whiteout.

Part 3A: Yes / No questions

Is <u>this</u> <u>a pencil sharpener</u>?

✓ **Yes, it is.** This **is** a pencil sharpener.

✗ **No, it isn't.** This **isn't** a pencil sharpener.

Is <u>that</u> <u>some tape</u>?

✓ **Yes, it is.** That **is** some tape.

✗ **No, it isn't.** That **isn't** some tape.

 **Winner's Tip!** Important: this / that

Part 3B: Fill in the blanks

1. Is this _____?
   Yes, it _____. This _____ _____.

2. _____ that _____?
   No, _____ isn't. _____ isn't _____.

3. _____ this _____?
   No, _____ _____. _____ isn't _____.

4. Is _____ _____?
   Yes, _____ is. That _____ _____.

Part 4A: Verb of the day

buy / buys – bought – buying – bought (купувати)

Every month, I <u>buy</u> a new eraser.

On weekends, he <u>buys</u> pencils and pens.

Yesterday, we <u>bought</u> some new glue.

He is <u>buying</u> some whiteout right now.

I have never <u>bought</u> a good ruler.

Part 4B: Verb Practice

1. Every Saturday, I _____ a new pen.
2. On Thursdays, she _____ markers and tape.
3. Every year, he _____ a new pencil sharpener.
4. Last night, they _____ a few pencils.
5. Last week, I _____ a great new marker.
6. Yesterday, you _____ two rulers.
7. Right now, he is _____ some glue.
8. They are _____ ten crayons right now.
9. I have never _____ a great pencil case.
10. We have _____ pens from that store many times.

Part 5A: Phonics Practice

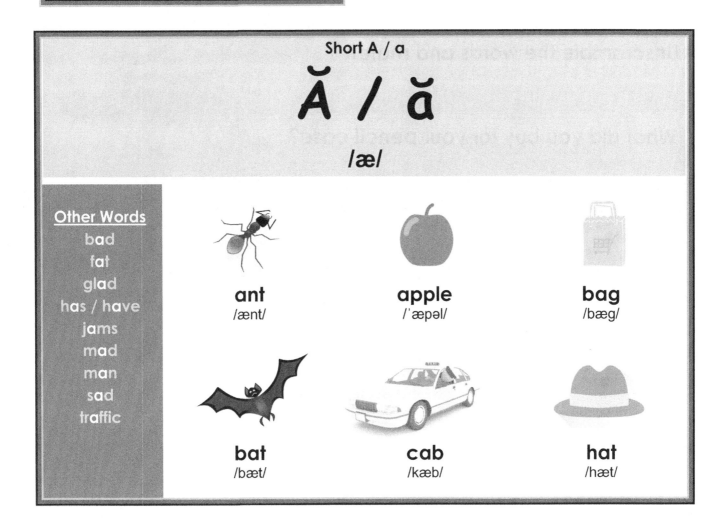

Short A / a

Ă / ă

/æ/

Other Words
bad
fat
glad
has / have
jams
mad
man
sad
traffic

ant
/ænt/

apple
/ˈæpəl/

bag
/bæg/

bat
/bæt/

cab
/kæb/

hat
/hæt/

Part 5B: Write and read

1. Gl__d h__t m__n h__s s__d b__ts.

2. __pple b__gs h__ve f__t __nts.

3. B__d c__bs h__ve m__d tr__ffic j__ms.

Unscramble the words and match

What did you buy for your pencil case?

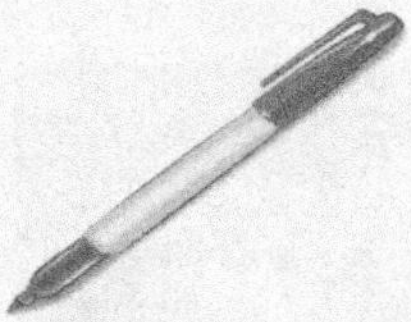

npe   _pen_

sarere   _____

cnlpei   _____

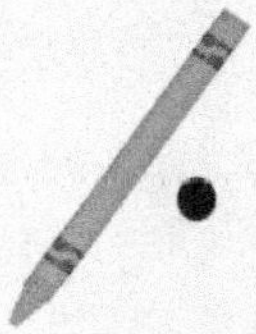

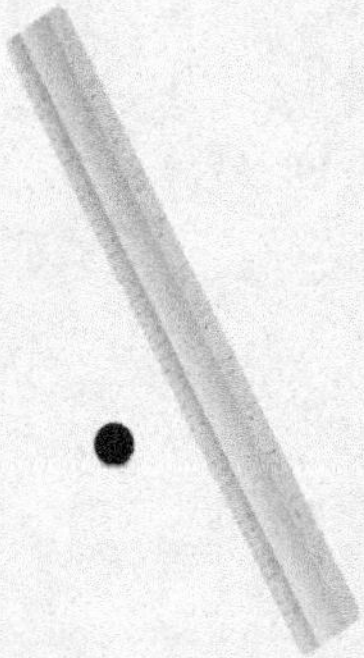

ienpcl rpnheears   _____

lerur   _____

ptea   _____

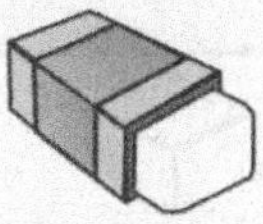

rkemra   _____

oycarn   _____

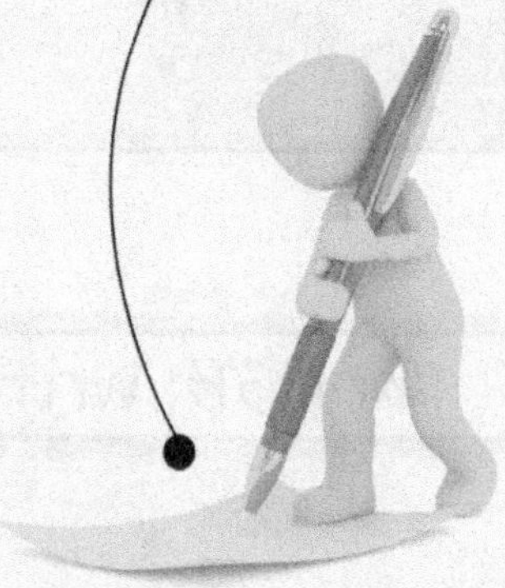

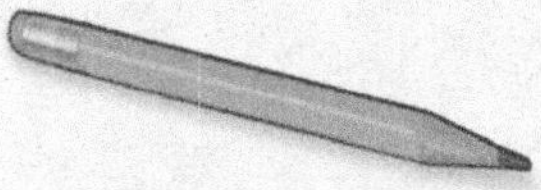

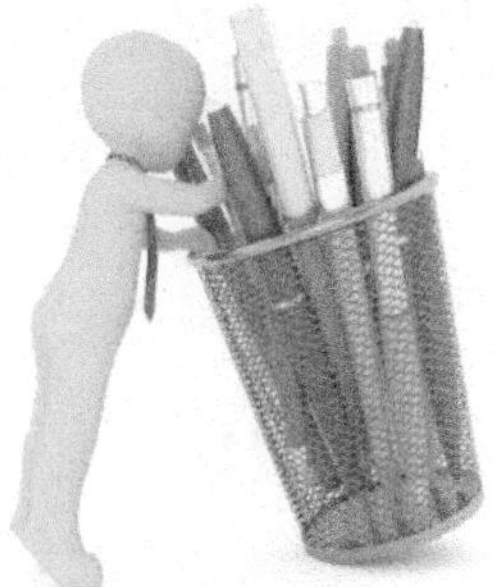

What did you not buy for your pencil case?

ulge   _____

tutiohwe   _____

I didn't buy _____ and _____ .

Lesson 2 In the classroom

в класі

Part 1A: Learn the words

1. **chair**
   стілець
2. **blackboard**
   класна дошка
3. **poster**
   плакат
4. **globe**
   глобус
5. **clock**
   годинник

6. **desk**
   стіл
7. **whiteboard**
   біла дошка
8. **bookshelf**
   книжкова полиця
9. **computer**
   комп'ютер
10. **book**
    книга

 Practice speaking: "стілець" is "_chair_" in English!

Part 1B: Write the words

Write the missing letters!   Write x 1   Write x 2

1. b _ a _ k _ o _ r _   _____   _____
2. _ o _ k   _____   _____
3. b _ o _ s _ e _ f   _____   _____
4. _ h _ i _   _____   _____
5. c _ o _ k   _____   _____
6. _ o _ p _ t _ r   _____   _____
7. d _ s _   _____   _____
8. _ l _ b _   _____   _____
9. p _ s _ e _   _____   _____
10. _ h _ t _ b _ a _ d _____   _____

Part 2A: Ask a question

What are <u>these</u>?

✓ **These** are <u>books</u>. **They are not** <u>computers</u>.

What are <u>those</u>?

✓ **Those** are <u>whiteboards</u>. **They aren't** <u>blackboards</u>.

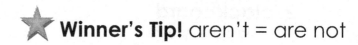 **Winner's Tip!** aren't = are not

Part 2B: Fill in the blanks

1. What are _____?
   These _____ posters. _____ aren't _____.

2. _____ are those?
   _____ are _____. They _____ _____.

3. _____ are _____?
   These _____ bookshelves. They _____ _____ _____.

4. _____ are _____?
   Those are _____. _____ _____ _____.

Are <u>these</u> <u>clock</u>s?

✓ **Yes, they are.** These **are** clocks.

✗ **No, they aren't.** These **aren't** clocks.

Are <u>those</u> <u>globe</u>s?

✓ **Yes, they are.** Those **are** globes.

✗ **No, they aren't.** Those **aren't** globes.

 Winner's Tip! Important: these / those

1. Are these _____?
   Yes, they _____. They _____ _____.

2. _____ those _____?
   No, _____ aren't. _____ aren't _____.

3. _____ these _____?
   No, _____ _____. _____ aren't _____.

4. Are _____ _____?
   Yes, _____ are. Those _____ _____.

Part 4A: Verb of the day

look / looks – looked – looking – looked (дивитися)

Every morning, I <u>look</u> at the blackboard.

On Fridays, she <u>looks</u> at the clock.

Yesterday, we <u>looked</u> at some posters.

She is <u>looking</u> at the bookshelf now.

I have never <u>looked</u> at his desk.

Part 4B: Verb Practice

1. Every Monday, I _____ for my books.
2. On Wednesdays, she _____ at her computer.
3. Every Sunday, he _____ for places on his globe.
4. Last class, they _____ at the blackboard.
5. Last weekend, I _____ for a new desk for my room.
6. This morning, we _____ on the bookshelf.
7. Right now, he is _____ under the chair.
8. We are _____ in the classroom right now.
9. She has never _____ at the whiteboard before.
10. You have _____ at your computer all day.

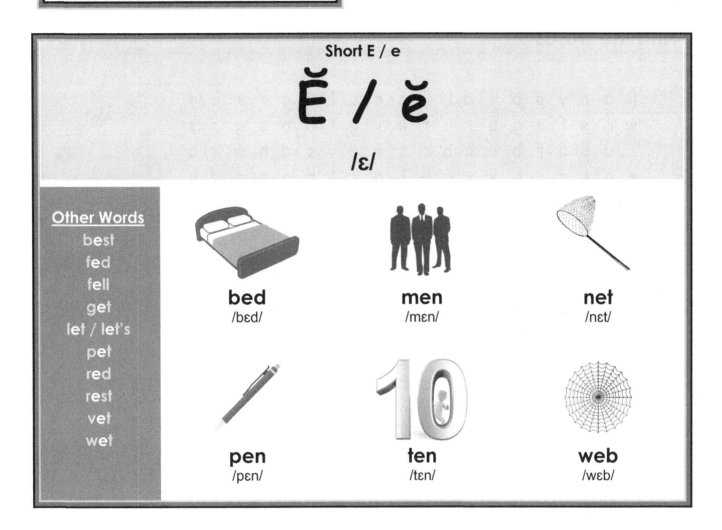

Short E / e

Ĕ / ĕ

/ɛ/

Other Words
best
fed
fell
get
let / let's
pet
red
rest
vet
wet

bed
/bɛd/

men
/mɛn/

net
/nɛt/

pen
/pɛn/

ten
/tɛn/

web
/wɛb/

Part 5B: Write and read

1. R__d n__ts f__ll on b__st m__n.

2. W__t v__ts l__t f_d p__ts g_t r__st.

3. L__t's g_t t_n w__b p__ns.

Find the words

```
l a n y p b y d l e r c c l m g v w e o
w r x f q g u l a f u i g l o b e g s s
i u p g f b i r b c c e v y s d h w z b
n o l o p o x y e b l a c k b o a r d n
n b k a d a s h g z f j r y p f z i h r
e m k s j m l b s r c e i f t p l n t s
r l w f f y m o f t t g u x f n k t x v
s m h k v y z o q s m x c h a i r h k o
e e i e m x w k o o p d b h b d a e s w
n p t v t p y p i y x o n e o y h c w e
g b e b l n o j x t r m w x o w j l u z
l r b x n b l j e c c l o c k d k a y q
i m o x w w k o r o o j u z s f r s d v
s x a i j w x z u m b r h u h f m s q m
h r r a u u h i n p s o d k e b e r w a
u p d k u r t o h u k p e h l a h o a j
v f s a m t v b k t j v s q f b b o v f
w f y w w b g x b e w p k u o w n m l o
n g t n k o s o h r c p i o p b d t i s
k h f p a y z t w m g u f l a g c g o c
```

chair	whiteboard
blackboard	desk
poster	bookshelf
globe	computer
clock	book

моя родина

Part 1A: Learn the words

1. **mother**
   мати
2. **sister**
   сестра
3. **aunt**
   тітка
4. **cousin**
   двоюрідна сестра / двоюрідний брат
5. **grandmother**
   бабуся

6. **father**
   батько
7. **brother**
   брат
8. **uncle**
   дядько
9. **niece / nephew**
   племінниця / племінник
10. **grandfather**
    дідусь

 Practice speaking: "мати" is "_mother_" in English!

Part 1B: Write the words

Write the missing letters!   Write x 1   Write x 2

1. m__t__e__   _____   _____
2. s__s__e__   _____   _____
3. __u__t   _____   _____
4. c__u__i__   _____   _____
5. g__a__d__ot__er   _____   _____
6. __a__h__r   _____   _____
7. b__o__h__r   _____   _____
8. __n__l__   _____   _____
9. n__e__e / __e__h__w   _____   _____
10. __r__n__f__t__e__   _____   _____

Who is <u>she</u>?

✓ She **is my <u>mother</u>. She is not my <u>aunt</u>.**

Who is <u>he</u>?

✓ He **is my <u>uncle</u>. He isn't my <u>father</u>.**

 Winner's Tip! Remember: isn't = is not

Part 2B: Fill in the blanks

1. Who is _____?
   She _____ my sister. _____ is not my _____.

2. _____ is he?
   _____ is _____ brother. He is _____ my uncle.

3. _____ is _____?
   She _____ my cousin. She _____ my _____.

4. _____ is _____?
   He is _____ grandfather. He _____ my _____.

Is <u>she</u> your <u>grandmother</u>?

✓ **Yes,** she **is.** She **is my** grandmother.
✗ **No,** she **isn't.** She **isn't my** grandmother.

Is <u>he</u> your <u>grandfather</u>?

✓ **Yes,** he **is.** He **is my** grandfather.
✗ **No,** he **isn't.** He **isn't my** grandfather.

Part 3B: Fill in the blanks

1. Is he your _____?
   Yes, he _____. He is my _____.

2. _____ she _____ mother?
   No, _____ isn't. She _____ my _____.

3. _____ he your _____?
   No, he _____. _____ isn't _____ brother.

4. Is _____ _____ niece?
   Yes, _____ is. She _____ _____ niece.

see / sees – saw – seeing – seen (бачити)

Every day, I <u>see</u> my family at breakfast.

On weekends, he <u>sees</u> his uncle at home.

Yesterday, we <u>saw</u> your brother at school.

She is <u>seeing</u> a doctor right now.

I have never <u>seen</u> that action movie.

Part 4B: Verb Practice

1. Every day, I _____ his grandfather.

2. On Tuesdays, she _____ my aunt and her dog.

3. Every Friday, he _____ his friends.

4. Last night, they _____ a TV show.

5. Last week, I _____ his brother at school.

6. Yesterday, you _____ my uncle at the store.

7. Right now, he is _____ a movie.

8. They are _____ a doctor right now.

9. I have never _____ his family before.

10. We have _____ that show many times.

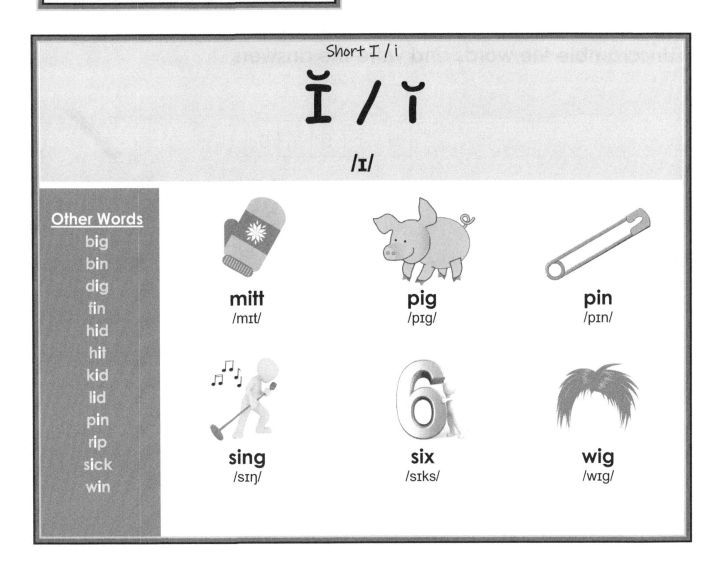

Short I / i

Ĭ / Ĭ

/ɪ/

Other Words
big
bin
dig
fin
hid
hit
kid
lid
pin
rip
sick
win

mitt
/mɪt/

pig
/pɪg/

pin
/pɪn/

sing
/sɪŋ/

six
/sɪks/

wig
/wɪg/

Part 5B: Write and read

1. S__x b__g p__gs in w__gs s__ng h__ts.

2. S__ck k__d h__d m__tt r__ps.

3. Jill w__ns p__ns in d__gging b__n l__ds.

Unscramble the words and write the answers

n	i	e	c	e

1. einec _niece_

2. istrse _____

3. lucne _____

4. usconi _____

5. ednorhatmgr _____

6. tmheor _____

7. tanu

_____

8. weepnh

_____

9. hfraet _____

10. rebotrh _____

11. frdarhanteg _____

Lesson 4 — Shapes

фігури

Part 1A: Learn the words

1. **square**
квадрат

2. **circle**
коло

3. **star**
зірка

4. **heart**
серце

5. **octagon**
восьмикутник

6. **triangle**
трикутник

7. **rectangle**
прямокутник

8. **oval**
овал

9. **diamond**
ромб

10. **pentagon**
п'ятикутник

 Practice speaking: "квадрат" is "<u>square</u>" in English!

Part 1B: Write the words

Write the missing letters!   Write x 1   Write x 2

1. c _ r _ l _   _____   _____
2. _ v _ l   _____   _____
3. t _ i _ n _ l _   _____   _____
4. _ q _ a _ e   _____   _____
5. p _ n _ a _ o _ _   _____   _____
6. _ t _ r   _____   _____
7. r _ c _ a _ g _ e   _____   _____
8. _ _ c _ a _ o _ _   _____   _____
9. d _ a _ o _ d   _____   _____
10. _ _ e _ r _ _   _____   _____

19

Part 2A: Ask a question

How many <u>squares</u> are there?

✓ **There is one** square.

How many <u>circles</u> are there?

✓ **There are <u>four</u> circle**s. **There aren't <u>five</u> circle**s.

 Winner's Tip! Remember: aren't = are not

Part 2B: Fill in the blanks

1. How _____ ovals are _____?
   There _____ six _____.

2. _____ many _____ are _____?
   _____ are _____ hearts.

3. _____ _____ _____ are _____?
   _____ is _____ _____.

4. _____ _____ triangles _____ _____?
   There _____ _____ _____.

Is there one <u>star</u>?

✓ **Yes, there is. There's one** star.

✗ **No, there is not. There isn't one** star.

Are there <u>seven</u> <u>hearts</u>?

✓ **Yes, there are. There are seven** hearts.

✗ **No, there aren't. There aren't seven** hearts.

 Winner's Tip! there's = there is

Part 3B: Fill in the blanks

1. Are there _____ _____?
   Yes, there _____. There _____ two octagons.

2. _____ there one _____?
   No, _____ isn't. There _____ _____ star.

3. _____ there _____ _____?
   No, _____ _____. There aren't four rectangles.

4. Are _____ _____ _____?
   Yes, _____ are. There are _____ pentagons.

Part 4A: Verb of the day

find / finds – found – finding – found (знаходити)

Every evening, we <u>find</u> stars in the sky.

Sometimes, she <u>finds</u> circles on her desk.

Yesterday, we <u>found</u> a blue diamond.

She is <u>finding</u> a triangle right now.

I have never <u>found</u> an octagon.

Part 4B: Verb Practice

1. Every day, we _____ shapes around the room.
2. On many days, he _____ circles on the floor.
3. Every night, she _____ bright stars.
4. Last class, we _____ a pentagon in a picture.
5. Last weekend, I _____ an octagon-shaped room.
6. This morning, they _____ a heart someone drew.
7. Right now, she is _____ triangle-shaped food.
8. I'm _____ a pencil to draw a big rectangle.
9. He has never _____ an oval-shaped eraser.
10. She has _____ many diamonds in the game.

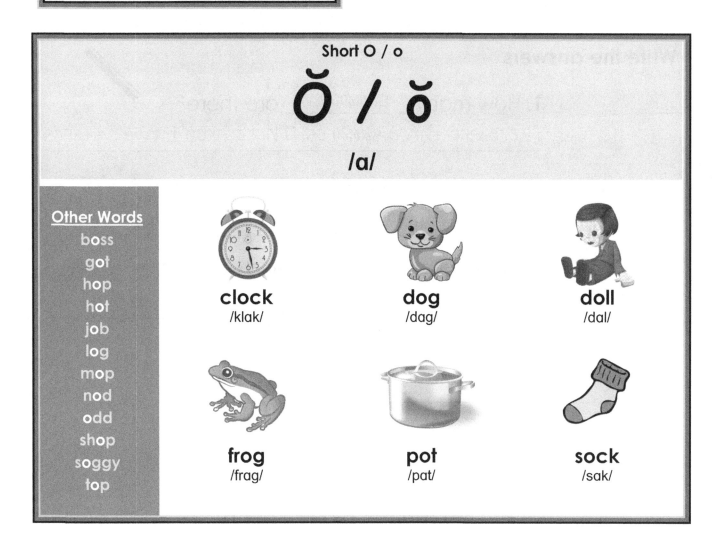

Short O / o

Ŏ / ŏ

/a/

Other Words
boss
got
hop
hot
job
log
mop
nod
odd
shop
soggy
top

clock
/klak/

dog
/dag/

doll
/dal/

frog
/frag/

pot
/pat/

sock
/sak/

Part 5B: Write and read

1. S__ggy fr__gs h__p on h__t p__t t__ps.

2. B__ss d__lls g__t n__dding d__gs __dd j__bs.

3. Tom m__pped Jon's sh__p with s__cks.

Write the answers

1. How many ___squares___ are there?
There are three squares. There aren't two squares.

2. How many _____ are there?
_____

3. How many _____ are there?
_____

4. How many _____ are there?
_____

Write the questions

1. Are there six stars?
Yes, there are. There are six ___stars___.

2. _____
No, there aren't. There aren't two _____.

3. _____
Yes, there are. There are four _____.

4. _____
Yes, there are. There are five _____.

The two other shapes are _____ and _____.

Lesson 5 At the toy store

у магазині іграшок

Part 1A: Learn the words

1. **an airplane**
   літак
2. **a ball**
   м'яч
3. **some blocks**
   конструктор
4. **a board game**
   настільна гра
5. **a car**
   машинка

6. **a dinosaur**
   динозавр
7. **a doll**
   лялька
8. **a jump rope**
   скакалка
9. **a robot**
   робот
10. **a teddy bear**
    плюшевий ведмедик

 Practice speaking: "лялька " is "_doll_" in English!

Part 1B: Write the words

Write the missing letters!   Write x 1   Write x 2

1. a_r_l_n__   _____   _____
2. _a_l   _____   _____
3. b_o_k__   _____   _____
4. _o_r_ g_m_   _____   _____
5. _a_   _____   _____
6. d_n_s_u__   _____   _____
7. _o_l   _____   _____
8. j_m__ r_p__   _____   _____
9. _o_o__   _____   _____
10. t_d_y _e_r   _____   _____

Part 2A: Ask a question

What do <u>you</u> have?

✓ **I have <u>a doll</u>. I don't have <u>a teddy bear</u>.**

What does <u>he</u> have?

✓ **He has <u>a board game</u>. He doesn't have <u>a car</u>.**

 Winner's Tip! he / she / it answer with "has"

Part 2B: Fill in the blanks

1. What _____ she _____?
   _____ has _____. She _____ have a car.

2. _____ do _____ have?
   We _____ _____. We _____ have a ball.

3. What _____ _____ _____?
   They _____ some blocks. They don't have _____.

4. _____ _____ _____ _____?
   He _____ a dinosaur. He doesn't _____ _____.

Do <u>you</u> have <u>a dinosaur?</u>

✓ **Yes, I do. I have** a dinosaur.

✗ **No, I do not. I don't have** a dinosaur.

Does <u>she</u> have <u>an airplane?</u>

✓ **Yes,** she **does.** She **has** an airplane.

✗ **No,** she **does not.** She **doesn't have** an airplane.

 Winner's Tip! don't = do not / doesn't = does not

1. _____ you _____ some blocks?
   Yes, I do. _____ _____ _____.

2. _____ she _____ a teddy bear?
   No, _____ _____. She _____ a jump rope.

3. _____ they _____ a car?
   No, _____ _____. _____ don't have a car.

4. Does _____ have _____?
   Yes, _____ does. He _____ _____.

Part 4A: Verb of the day

borrow / borrows – borrowed – borrowing – borrowed (позичати, брати)

Every week, I <u>borrow</u> a car from him.

Sometimes, she <u>borrows</u> his dinosaur toy.

Yesterday, I <u>borrowed</u> his airplane.

He is <u>borrowing</u> a robot right now.

She has never <u>borrowed</u> anything.

Part 4B: Verb Practice

1. Every Monday, I _____ my friend's blocks.
2. On Tuesdays, he _____ board games from me.
3. Every day, she _____ my jump rope.
4. Last time, we _____ his toy dinosaur.
5. Last week, they _____ some dolls to play with.
6. Yesterday, he _____ my favorite robot.
7. Right now, she is _____ a ball to play a game.
8. They are _____ a car for their vacation.
9. He has never _____ an airplane before.
10. You have _____ my teddy bear many times.

Part 5A: Phonics Practice

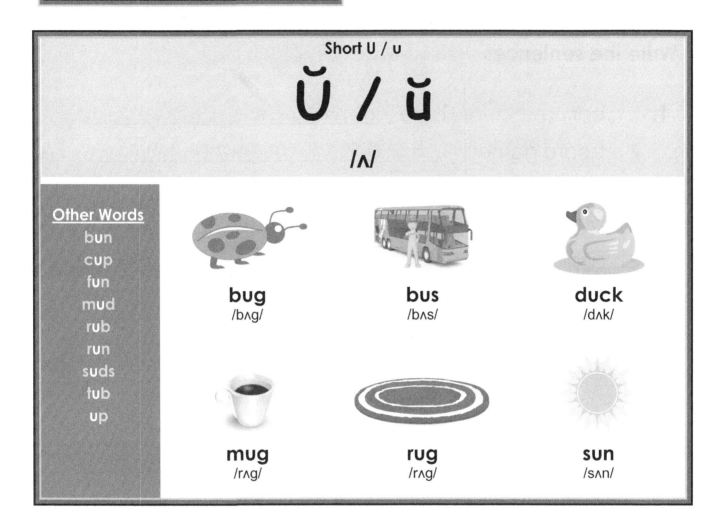

Short U / u

Ŭ / ŭ

/ʌ/

Other Words
bun
cup
fun
mud
rub
run
suds
tub
up

bug
/bʌg/

bus
/bʌs/

duck
/dʌk/

mug
/rʌg/

rug
/rʌg/

sun
/sʌn/

Part 5B: Write and read

1. One f__n b__g r__ns on some r__gs.

2. F__n t__b d__cks r__b s__ds on m__d.

3. A m__g, b__n, and b__s __nder the s__n.

Write the sentences

1. ✓ car
   ✗ board game

1. He _has a car._
   He doesn't have a board game.

2. ✓ ball
   ✗ airplane

2. We _____

3. ✓ teddy bear
   ✗ blocks

3. She _____

Yes or no?

1. Do you have a dinosaur?
   Yes, I do. I have a dinosaur.

2. Does she have a robot?
   _____

3. Does he have a jump rope?
   _____

Write the correct answer next to the letter "A"

A: ___ **1.** Is that a _____? Yes, it is. _____ is a marker.
a) marker / That's   **b)** markers / That
c) marker / That   **d)** marker / It's

A: ___ **2.** What are _____? Those are books. They _____ posters.
a) those / aren't   **b)** those / are
c) these / don't   **d)** books / 're not

A: ___ **3.** How many _____ _____ there? There is one triangle.
a) triangle / is   **b)** triangles / are
c) triangles / find   **d)** triangles / does

A: ___ **4.** Who is he? He is my _____. He _____ my uncle.
a) brother / isn't   **b)** father / 's
c) uncle / been   **d)** brother / looks

A: ___ **5.** What is this? _____ is a pen. It is not a _____.
a) This / eraser   **b)** It / pen
c) That / ruler   **d)** This / pencil

A: ___ **6.** What do you _____? I have a star. I _____ have a circle.
a) has / don't   **b)** have / doesn't
c) have / don't   **d)** had / can't

A: ___ **7.** _____ those clocks? Yes, _____ are. Those are clocks.
a) Are / these   **b)** Is / it
c) Do / those   **d)** Are / they

A: ___ **8.** Is that some _____? No, it _____. That isn't some whiteout.
a) glue / can't   **b)** whiteout / isn't
c) tape / doesn't   **d)** whiteout / doesn't

A: ___ **9.** Do you _____ a doll? Yes, I _____. I have a doll.
a) have / have   **b)** has / has
c) has / have   **d)** have / do

A: ___ **10.** Is she your _____? No, she isn't. She isn't my _____.
a) cousin / cousin
b) father / father
c) sister / family
d) nephew / nephew

A: ___ **11.** Right now, she is _____ her keys.
a) find
b) finds
c) finding
d) found

A: ___ **12.** What does he _____? He has a car. He doesn't _____ a ball.
a) has / has
b) have / hold
c) have / have
d) having / have

A: ___ **13.** Yesterday, we _____ your brother at school.
a) sees
b) saw
c) see
d) seen

A: ___ **14.** _____ she have a dinosaur? No, she _____. She doesn't have a dinosaur.
a) Do / don't
b) Has / hasn't
c) Doesn't / does
d) Does / doesn't

A: ___ **15.** What are _____? Those are _____. They aren't chairs.
a) these / bookshelves
b) those / desk
c) those / desks
d) this / globes

A: ___ **16.** Are there seven _____? Yes, there are. There are seven _____.
a) ovals / ovals
b) oval / ovals
c) ovals / oval
d) oval / shapes

A: ___ **17.** Every week, she _____ new pencils and erasers.
a) buy
b) buys
c) buyed
d) buying

A: ___ **18.** Sometimes, I _____ money from my aunt.
a) borrowing
b) borrows
c) have borrow
d) borrow

Answers on page 257

Lesson 6 Food & drinks

їжа та напої

Part 1A: Learn the words

1. **cake**
   торт
2. **cheese**
   сир
3. **milk**
   молоко
4. **tea**
   чай
5. **soda**
   газована вода

6. **pizza**
   піца
7. **water**
   вода
8. **juice**
   сік
9. **coffee**
   кава
10. **pie**
    пиріг

 Practice speaking: "торт" is "_cake_" in English!

Part 1B: Write the words

Write the missing letters!   Write x 1   Write x 2

1. c _ k _ _   _____   _____
2. _ h _ e _ e   _____   _____
3. c _ f _ e _   _____   _____
4. _ u _ c _   _____   _____
5. m _ l _   _____   _____
6. _ i _   _____   _____
7. p _ z _ a   _____   _____
8. _ o _ a   _____   _____
9. _ e _ _   _____   _____
10. w _ t _ r   _____   _____

What do <u>you</u> want?

✓ I want some <u>cake</u>. I don't want any <u>pie</u>.

What does <u>he</u> want?

✓ He wants some <u>tea</u>. He doesn't want any <u>soda</u>.

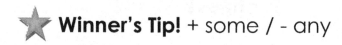 **Winner's Tip!** + some / - any

Part 2B: Fill in the blanks

1. What _____ you _____?
   We _____ some _____. We don't want any pie.

2. _____ does _____ _____?
   He _____ some tea. He _____ want any soda.

3. _____ _____ she _____?
   She _____ _____ pie. She doesn't want any cake.

4. _____ _____ _____ _____?
   They _____ _____ _____. They _____
   want any _____.

Part 3A: Yes / No questions

Do <u>you</u> want some <u>water</u>?

✓ **Yes, I do. I want some** water.

✗ **No, I do not. I don't want any** water.

Does <u>she</u> want some <u>juice</u>?

✓ **Yes,** she **does. She wants some** juice.

✗ **No,** she **does not. She doesn't want any** juice.

 Winner's Tip! don't = do not / doesn't = does not

Part 3B: Fill in the blanks

1. Does he _____ some _____?
   Yes, he _____. He _____ _____ juice.

2. Do _____ want _____ _____?
   No, I do not. I _____ want _____ soda.

3. _____ she _____ _____ _____?
   Yes, she _____. She _____ _____ milk.

4. Do _____ _____ _____ tea?
   No, we don't. We _____ _____ _____ tea.

want / wants – wanted – wanting – wanted (хотіти)

Sometimes, I <u>want</u> some milk and pie.

Every morning, he <u>wants</u> some coffee.

Last night, we <u>wanted</u> some pizza to eat.

(He is <u>wanting</u> to ask you for some cake.)*

I have never <u>wanted</u> to drink soda.

*less common, polite form

Part 4B: Verb Practice

1. Every breakfast, I _____ a cup of coffee.

2. On Fridays, she _____ pizza for dinner.

3. Every evening, he _____ some soda to drink.

4. Last time, they _____ some juice and soda.

5. Last weekend, I _____ to eat some cake.

6. This morning, we _____ some tea at breakfast.

7. Last night, he _____ to drink some milk.

8. Right now, he is _____ to ask for a drink.*

9. She has never _____ any water with her food.

10. You have _____ some pie for a long time.

Long A / a

Ā / ā

/eɪ/

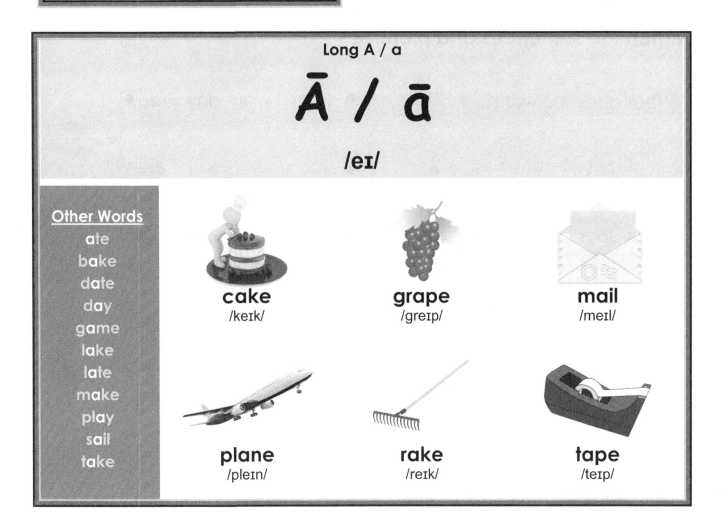

Other Words
ate
bake
date
day
game
lake
late
make
play
sail
take

cake
/keɪk/

grape
/greɪp/

mail
/meɪl/

plane
/pleɪn/

rake
/reɪk/

tape
/teɪp/

1. May __te gr__pe c__ke by the l__ke.

2. Dale t__kes t__ped r__kes on pl__nes.

3. Jay pl__ys g__mes and m__kes m__il l__te.

Match the sentences and pictures

What does she want? ●   ● I don't want any soda. ●

Do you want some cake? ●   ● Yes, they do. ●

What does he want? ●   ● She wants some tea. ● ●

Does she want some pie? ●   ● No, he doesn't. ●

What do they want? ●   ● Yes, I do. ●

Does he want some cheese? ●   ● He wants some water. ●

Do they want some pizza? ●   ● No, she doesn't. ●

What do you want? ●   ● They don't want any coffee. ●

Lesson 7 Vegetables

овочі

Part 1A: Learn the words

1. **pumpkin**
   гарбуз
2. **potato**
   картопля
3. **carrot**
   морква
4. **asparagus**
   спаржа
5. **broccoli**
   брокколі

6. **corn**
   кукурудза
7. **cabbage**
   капуста
8. **spinach**
   шпинат
9. **mushroom**
   гриб
10. **onion**
   цибуля

 Practice speaking: "кукурудза " is "_corn_" in English!

Part 1B: Write the words

Write the missing letters!   Write x 1   Write x 2

1. a__p__r__g__s   _____   _____
2. __r__c__o__i   _____   _____
3. c__b__a__e   _____   _____
4. __a__r__t   _____   _____
5. c__r__   _____   _____
6. __u__h__o__m   _____   _____
7. o__i__n   _____   _____
8. __o__a__o   _____   _____
9. p__m__k__n   _____   _____
10. __p__n__c__   _____   _____

What do <u>you</u> want to eat?

✓ I **want to eat some <u>broccoli</u>.**

✗ I **don't want to eat any <u>onion</u>.**

What does <u>she</u> want to eat?

✓ She **wants to eat some <u>carrot</u>.**

✗ She **doesn't want to eat any <u>potato</u>.**

 Winner's Tip! he / she / it verb+ "**s**"

Part 2B: Fill in the blanks

1. what _____ you _____ to eat?

   I _____ to eat some _____.

2. _____ _____ he want _____ eat?

   He _____ to eat _____ _____.

3. _____ does _____ _____ to _____?

   She _____ want _____ eat any _____.

4. what _____ they _____ _____ _____?

   They don't _____ _____ _____ any _____.

Do _you_ want to eat some _cabbage_?

✓ **Yes, I do. I want to eat some** cabbage.
✗ **No, I don't. I don't want to eat any** cabbage.

Does _he_ want to eat some _corn_?

✓ **Yes,** he **does. He wants to eat some** corn.
✗ **No,** he **doesn't. He doesn't want to eat any** corn.

 Winner's Tip! Remember: + some / - any

Part 3B: Fill in the blanks

1. Do you _____ to _____ some _____?
   Yes, I do. I _____ to eat _____ mushroom.

2. _____ he _____ to eat some _____?
   No, he _____. He _____ want to eat any corn.

3. _____ they want to _____ _____ pumpkin?
   No, they _____. They don't want to eat any _____.

4. Does _____ want to eat some _____?
   Yes, he _____. He _____ to eat _____ onion.

cook / cooks – cooked – cooking – cooked (готувати)

Every afternoon, I <u>cook</u> some broccoli.

Often, he <u>cooks</u> onion for his breakfast.

Yesterday, we <u>cooked</u> a lot of corn.

She is <u>cooking</u> some pumpkin for dinner.

We have never <u>cooked</u> any asparagus.

Part 4B: Verb Practice

1. Every day, I _____ vegetables for my lunch.

2. On Mondays, he _____ asparagus for his meals.

3. Every Saturday, he _____ corn with his friends.

4. Last night, we _____ some broccoli and potato.

5. Last weekend, I _____ some spinach and onion.

6. Yesterday, he _____ a big meal for everyone.

7. Right now, he is _____ a really big pumpkin.

8. They are _____ many carrots right now.

9. He has never _____ cabbage well before.

10. I have _____ mushroom many times before now.

Part 5A: Phonics Practice

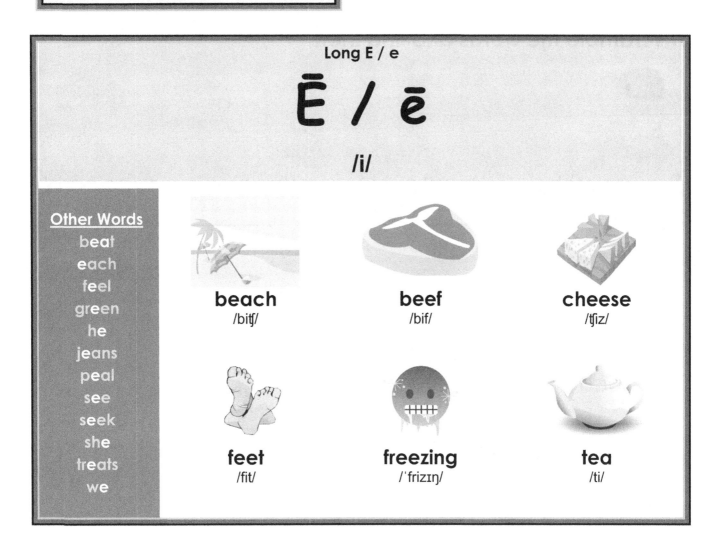

Long E / e

Ē / ē

/i/

Other Words
beat
each
feel
green
he
jeans
peal
see
seek
she
treats
we

beach
/bitʃ/

beef
/bif/

cheese
/tʃiz/

feet
/fit/

freezing
/ˈfrizɪŋ/

tea
/ti/

Part 5B: Write and read

1. M__an Pete __ats b__ef ch__ese tr__ats.

2. W__ s__e gr__en t__a tr__es s__ek s__as.

3. H__ b__ats fr__ezing f__et at __ach b__ach.

43

Unscramble the words and find them

 smmuoroh
<u>mushroom</u>

 nmpkpui
_____

 ottpoa
_____

 coiocrbl
_____

 bgabcae
_____

 inpcsah
_____

sarsupaga
_____

nooin
_____

rnoc
_____

rctora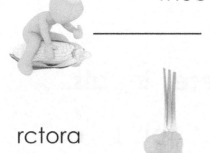
_____

```
z z d h q o z f m g e c g x j x g s
m i c p b c e g x r a l c n f j u z
y h n w s h z p o t r o i c j g z o
x h i c b x l o q r k r x d a y t w
x b e v e g e t a b l e s r o h p m
o r c w l x n a k a w q a a c t n s
f o a w d b o t q t r p d a r q s p
b c b j c e k o j f s g n x v q j o
t c b y f u f b c a h i x z z q y o
d o a n p v d z p c p s y a i i o n
x l g w i n n e r s e n g l i s h v
c i e y n g a g o q o f w k r b w z
t a u o p d m g n e m v o l j d t g
x a j o t u v s i m u s h r o o m f
c a r r o t h n o j y s z o k g x i
o v p u m p k i n k a v f z v a q b
r d i f a c h e f s h a t c p g m e
n a u q o h m t j a t t c k p s f x
```

Lesson 8 — Colors

кольори

Part 1A: Learn the words

1. **pink**
   рожевий
2. **red**
   червоний
3. **orange**
   помаранчевий
4. **yellow**
   жовтий
5. **green**
   зелений

6. **blue**
   синій
7. **purple**
   фіолетовий
8. **white**
   білий
9. **brown**
   коричневий
10. **black**
   чорний

 Practice speaking: "червоний" is "<u>red</u>" in English!

Part 1B: Write the words

Write the missing letters!   Write x 1   Write x 2

1. p__n__   _____   _____
2. __e__   _____   _____
3. o__a__g__   _____   _____
4. __e__l__w   _____   _____
5. g__e__n   _____   _____
6. __l__e   _____   _____
7. p__r__l__   _____   _____
8. __h__t__   _____   _____
9. b__o__n   _____   _____
10. __l__c__   _____   _____

What color do <u>you</u> like?

✓ I like <u>pink</u>, but I don't like <u>green</u>.

What color does <u>she</u> like?

✓ She likes <u>black</u>, but she doesn't like <u>orange</u>.

 Winner's Tip! "but" for contrast

Part 2B: Fill in the blanks

1. What _____ does _____ like?
   He _____ blue, but he _____ like _____.

2. What _____ do _____ like?
   They _____ yellow, but they _____ like _____.

3. _____ color _____ she _____?
   She _____ red, but she _____ _____ _____.

4. _____ color _____ _____ _____?
   I _____ pink, but I _____ _____ _____.

Do <u>you</u> like the color <u>red</u>?

✓ **Yes, I do. I like the color** red.
✗ **No, I don't. I don't like the color** red.

Does <u>he</u> like the color <u>blue</u>?

✓ **Yes, he does. He likes the color** blue.
✗ **No, he doesn't. He doesn't like the color** blue.

 Winner's Tip! (the color) = optional

1. _____ you _____ the color green?
   Yes, I do. I _____ the _____ _____.

2. _____ he _____ the color orange?
   No, he _____. He _____ like _____.

3. Do _____ like _____?
   No, I _____. I _____ _____ purple.

4. Does _____ like _____?
   Yes, she _____. She _____ the color _____.

draw / draws – drew – drawing – drawn (малювати)

I <u>draw</u> red apples every art class.

She usually <u>draws</u> with a black pencil.

Yesterday, she <u>drew</u> an orange carrot.

He is <u>drawing</u> a picture right now.

She has never <u>drawn</u> a purple car.

Part 4B: Verb Practice

1. Every evening, we _____ many different shapes.
2. On Fridays, she _____ lots of colorful pictures.
3. Sometimes, he _____ pictures of his family.
4. Yesterday, we _____ green dinosaurs for fun.
5. Last week, she _____ something in red crayon.
6. Earlier today, he _____ some vegetables.
7. Right now, she is _____ with her black pencil.
8. We are _____ in the classroom right now.
9. She has never _____ any food or drinks before.
10. I have _____ so many pictures this week.

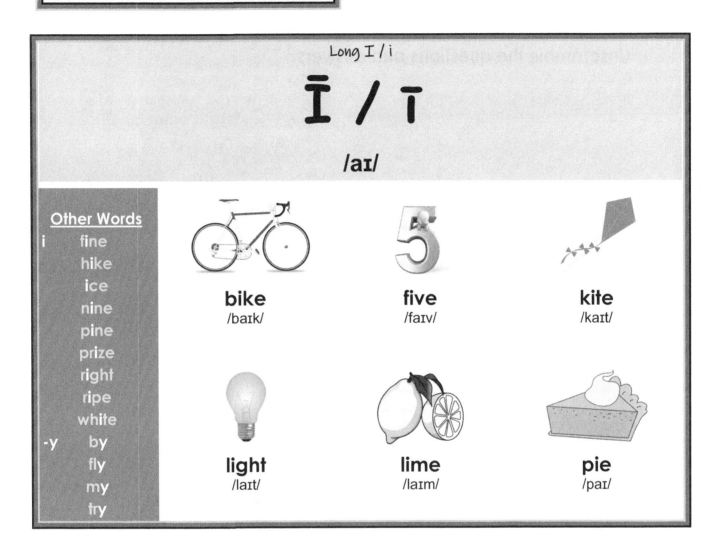

Long I / i

Ī / ī

/aɪ/

Other Words

i   fine
    hike
    ice
    nine
    pine
    prize
    right
    ripe
    white
-y   by
    fly
    my
    try

bike
/baɪk/

five
/faɪv/

kite
/kaɪt/

light
/laɪt/

lime
/laɪm/

pie
/paɪ/

Part 5B: Write and read

1. Tr__ m__ f__ve pr__zed r__pe l__me p__es.

2. F__nd n__ne r__ght s__zed b__ke l__ghts.

3. H__ke wh__te __ce to fly k__tes b__ p__nes.

Part 6: Fun review

Unscramble the questions and answers

he   does
color   like   What

purple   but   brown
likes   he   like
doesn't   He

What color does he like? _____

you   color
like   What   do

like   but   I
blue   red   like
I   don't

_____   _____

like   Do   color   the   black   you
black   I   like   the   do   I   color   Yes

_____
_____ ?

_____

she   color   the   like   Does   green
green   color   the   like   doesn't   No   she

_____
_____ ?

_____

50

Lesson 9 — At the fruit market

на фруктовому ринку

Part 1A: Learn the words

1. **apple**
   яблуко
2. **banana**
   банан
3. **cherry**
   вишня
4. **grape**
   виноград
5. **lemon**
   лимон

6. **orange**
   апельсин
7. **pear**
   груша
8. **pineapple**
   ананас
9. **strawberry**
   полуниця
10. **watermelon**
    кавун

 Practice speaking: "яблуко " is "_apple_" in English!

Part 1B: Write the words

Write the missing letters!   Write x 1   Write x 2

1. __p__l__ _____ _____
2. b__n__n__ _____ _____
3. __h__r__y _____ _____
4. g__a__e _____ _____
5. __e__o__ _____ _____
6. o__a__g__ _____ _____
7. __e__r _____ _____
8. p__n__a__p__e _____ _____
9. __t__a__b__r__y _____ _____
10. w__t__r__e__o__ _____ _____

Part 2A: Ask a question

What color is <u>this</u> <u>apple</u>?

✓ **This apple is <u>green</u>. It isn't <u>red</u>.**

What color are <u>these</u> <u>grape</u>s?

✓ **These grapes are <u>purple</u>. They aren't <u>pink</u>.**

 Winner's Tip! this, that / these, those

Part 2B: Fill in the blanks

1. _____ color are _____ bananas?
   Those _____ _____ brown. They aren't _____.

2. what _____ _____ these _____?
   _____ cherries are red. They _____ _____.

3. _____ _____ is _____ pineapple?
   This _____ is green. _____ isn't _____.

4. what _____ are _____ _____?
   Those pears _____ pink. _____ _____ _____.

Part 3A: Yes / No questions

Is <u>that</u> <u>banana</u> <u>yellow</u>?

✓ **Yes, it is. That's a yellow** banana.
✗ **No, it isn't. That isn't a yellow** banana.

Are <u>these</u> <u>strawberries</u> <u>red</u>?

✓ **Yes, they are. These are red** strawberries.
✗ **No, they aren't. These aren't red** strawberries.

 Winner's Tip! Plural: word ending -y becomes -ies

Part 3B: Fill in the blanks

1. Are these _____ orange?
   No, they _____. These _____ _____ lemons.

2. Is _____ watermelon _____?
   No, _____ isn't. This _____ a blue _____.

3. _____ those _____ black?
   No, _____ _____. _____ aren't black grapes.

4. Are _____ _____ _____?
   Yes, _____ are. These _____ _____ lemons.

need / needs – needed – needing – needed (потребувати)

Every day, I **need** to eat some fruit.

Sometimes, he **needs** orange juice.

Yesterday, I **needed** to buy apples.

She is **needing** more vitamin C.*

Lately, we have **needed** many things.

*needing = less common

Part 4B: Verb Practice

1. Every day, I _____ to eat more vegetables.
2. On Mondays, he _____ a coffee before work.
3. Every morning, she _____ to buy new pencils.
4. Last time, they _____ to get some strawberries.
5. Last month, I _____ a new chair for my classroom.
6. Yesterday, she _____ to call her brother and sister.
7. Right now, he is _____ some help with school.*
8. They are _____ happier teachers and students.*
9. He has never _____ many toys to have fun.
10. We have _____ some new books for a long time.

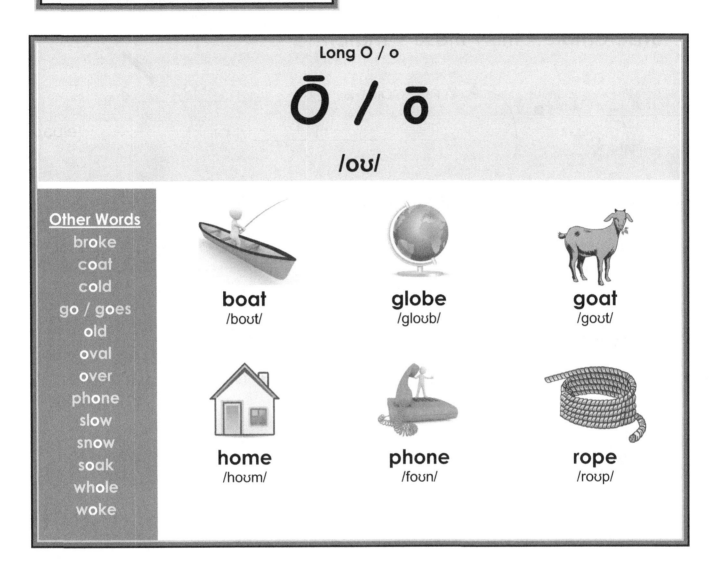

Long O / o

Ō / ō

/oʊ/

Other Words
broke
coat
cold
go / goes
old
oval
over
phone
slow
snow
soak
whole
woke

boat
/boʊt/

globe
/gloʊb/

goat
/goʊt/

home
/hoʊm/

phone
/foʊn/

rope
/roʊp/

Part 5B: Write and read

1. G__at's b__at g__es sl__w __ver the gl__be.

2. S__aked __ld r__pes br__ke c__ld sn__w.

3. The __val ph__ne w__ke the wh__le h__me.

Unscramble + this / these + match

What color is ___this___ ___apple___ ?

___This___ ___apple___ is pink.   [elpap]

What color are _____ _____ ?

_____ _____ are purple.   [rpsega]

What color are _____ _____?

_____ _____ are red.   [aresswerritb]

What color is _____ _____?

_____ _____ is brown.   [aplipneep]

What color is _____ _____?

_____ _____ is yellow.   [erap]

What color is _____ _____?

_____ _____ is green.   [naanba]

Lesson 10 Feelings

почуття

Part 1A: Learn the words

1. **sad**
   сумний
2. **tired**
   втомлений
3. **fine**
   в порядку
4. **bored**
   знуджений
5. **energetic**
   енергійний
6. **happy**
   щасливий
7. **sick**
   хворий
8. **angry**
   сердитий
9. **excited**
   збуджений
10. **frustrated**
    розчарований

 Practice speaking: "щасливий" is "_happy_" in English!

Part 1B: Write the words

Write the missing letters!   Write x 1   Write x 2

1. a__g__y   _____   _____
2. __o__e__   _____   _____
3. e__e__g__t__c   _____   _____
4. __x__i__e__   _____   _____
5. f__n__   _____   _____
6. __r__s__r__t__d   _____   _____
7. h__p__y   _____   _____
8. __a__   _____   _____
9. s__c__   _____   _____
10. __i__e__   _____   _____

57

How are <u>you</u> feeling right now?

✓ **Right now, I'm feeling <u>happy</u>. I'm not feeling <u>sad</u>.**

How is <u>he</u> feeling right now?

✓ **Right now, he's feeling <u>bored</u>. He's not feeling <u>excited</u>.**

⭐ **Winner's Tip!** you're not = you aren't / he's not = he isn't / she's not = she isn't / it's not = it isn't / we're not = we aren't / they're not = they aren't

Part 2B: Fill in the blanks

1. _____ are _____ feeling _____ now?
   Right now, I'm _____ sick. _____ not feeling fine.

2. _____ is _____ _____ right now?
   Right now, he's _____ excited. He's not feeling _____.

3. _____ is _____ _____ _____ now?
   She's feeling _____. She's _____ _____ angry.

4. _____ are _____ _____ _____ now?
   They're _____ tired. They're not _____ _____.

Part 3A: Yes / No questions

Are <u>you</u> feeling <u>angry</u> right now?

✓ **Yes, I am. I'm feeling** angry **right now.**

✗ **No, I'm not. I'm not feeling** angry **right now.**

Is <u>she</u> feeling <u>tired</u> right now?

✓ **Yes,** she **is.** She's **feeling** tired **right now.**

✗ **No,** she's **not.** She **isn't feeling** tired **right now.**

**Winner's Tip!** "right now" = optional

Part 3B: Fill in the blanks

1. Is she _____ energetic _____ now?
   Yes, she is. _____ _____ _____ right now.

2. Are you _____ _____ right _____?
   No, I'm not. _____ not _____ happy right now.

3. _____ they _____ sick _____ _____?
   No, they're not. They're not _____ _____ right now.

4. Is _____ _____ bored _____ _____?
   Yes, he is. He's _____ _____ right now.

think / thinks – thought – thinking – thought (думати)

Every day, I <u>think</u> of new ways to be happy.

Sometimes, he <u>thinks</u> angry thoughts.

Yesterday, we <u>thought</u> about what to eat.

She is <u>thinking</u> about her family right now.

I have never <u>thought</u> about his feelings.

Part 4B: Verb Practice

1. Each day, I _____ about what to eat for lunch.

2. On Wednesdays, she _____ of something to cook.

3. Every Tuesday, he _____ about his brother.

4. Yesterday, they _____ about their favorite toys.

5. Last week, we _____ of a way to fix the problem.

6. Earlier today, I _____ about my family.

7. Right now, he is _____ about watching a movie.

8. They are _____ about moving to a new house.

9. He has never _____ about that problem before.

10. You have _____ of many different examples.

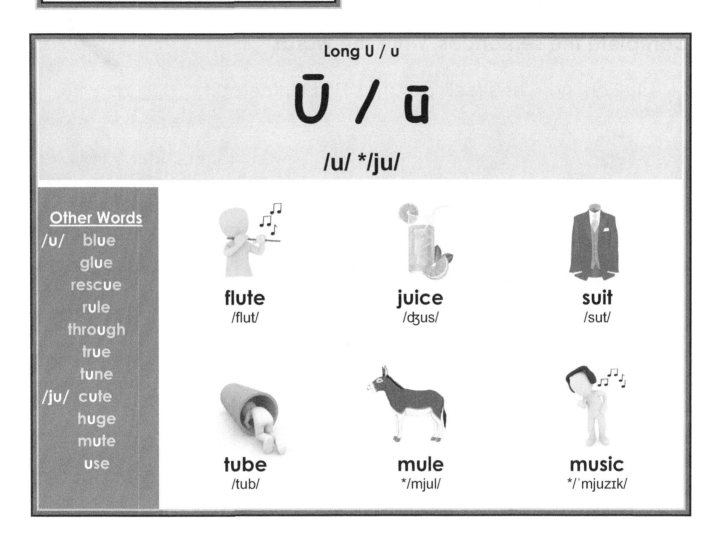

Long U / u

Ū / ū

/u/ */ju/

Other Words

/u/ blue
glue
rescue
rule
through
true
tune
/ju/ cute
huge
mute
use

flute
/flut/

juice
/dʒus/

suit
/sut/

tube
/tub/

mule
*/mjul/

music
*/ˈmjuzɪk/

Part 5B: Write and read

1. Tr__e s__it r__les resc__e bl__e j__ice.

2. Fl__te t__nes blew gl__e thro__gh t__bes.

*3. H__ge c__te m__les __se m__ted m__sic.

Part 6: Fun review

Complete the sentences, write the words

1. Right now, he's feeling s_*a*_d. He isn't feeling t_____d.

s____d   t____d   f___e   b___d   e_____c

2. Right now, she's feeling s____k. She's not feeling f_____d.

h____y   s____k   a____y   e_____d   f_____d

3. How are you feeling right now?

_____

62

Write the correct answer next to the letter "A"

A: ___ **1.** What does he _____ to eat? He _____ want to eat any corn.
a) wants / does   **b)** want / doesn't
c) wanting / don't   **d)** want / don't

A: ___ **2.** What color _____ they like? They like red, but they _____ like blue.
a) does / doesn't   **b)** do / doesn't
c) are / aren't   **d)** do / don't

A: ___ **3.** What color _____ these pears? These pears _____ red.
a) are / are   **b)** do / colored
c) is / color   **d)** are / color is

A: ___ **4.** What do you want? I want _____ tea. I don't want _____ coffee.
a) any / some   **b)** much / lots of
c) some / many   **d)** some / any

A: ___ **5.** Is he _____ sad right now? Yes, he _____. He's feeling sad.
a) feel / does   **b)** feels / feels
c) feeling / is   **d)** feeling / feeling

A: ___ **6.** _____ this lemon green? Yes, it is. _____ is a green lemon.
a) Does / It   **b)** Is / This
c) Do / It's   **d)** Are / These

A: ___ **7.** Last night, we _____ many different colors on the paper.
a) draw   **b)** drawing
c) drew   **d)** drawn

A: ___ **8.** _____ she want some pie? Yes, she does. She _____ some pie.
a) Do / want   **b)** Would / wanting
c) Does / wants   **d)** Does / want

A: ___ **9.** He is _____ some vegetables for lunch.
a) cooking   **b)** cook
c) cooked   **d)** cooks

A: ___ 10. _____ she like the color yellow? No, she _____. She doesn't like the color yellow.
a) Do / don't   **b)** Does / doesn't
c) Does / doesn't like   **d)** Does / don't like

A: ___ 11. Every day after work, he _____ to sleep.
a) want   **b)** wanting
c) has want   **d)** wants

A: ___ 12. Last weekend, I _____ to visit my sick friend.
a) need   **b)** needing
c) needs   **d)** needed

A: ___ 13. How is she _____ right now? Right now, _____ feeling excited.
a) feel / she is   **b)** felt / she
c) feeling / she's   **d)** feels / she has

A: ___ 14. Every month, he _____ about traveling around the world.
a) thinks   **b)** think
c) thinking   **d)** is thought

A: ___ 15. Do you _____ the color pink? Yes, I _____. I like the color pink.
a) like / like   **b)** liking / does
c) likes / do   **d)** like / do

A: ___ 16. Do _____ want to eat some onion? No, they _____. They don't want to eat any onion.
a) them / aren't   **b)** they / don't
c) we / doesn't   **d)** they / doesn't

A: ___ 17. How are _____ feeling right now? Right now, _____ feeling fine.
a) you / I can   **b)** we / we'll
c) they / they're   **d)** they / they'll

A: ___ 18. He really _____ _____ red onions for a long time.
a) hasn't / cooked   **b)** hasn't / cooking
c) didn't / cooked   **d)** doesn't / cooks

Answers on page 257

At the zoo

в зоопарку

Part 1A: Learn the words

1. **bear**
   ведмідь
2. **crocodile**
   крокодил
3. **elephant**
   слон
4. **giraffe**
   жирафа
5. **kangaroo**
   кенгуру

6. **lion**
   лев
7. **monkey**
   мавпа
8. **penguin**
   пінгвін
9. **rhino**
   носоріг
10. **tiger**
    тигр

 Practice speaking: "мавпа " is "<u>monkey</u>" in English!

Part 1B: Write the words

Write the missing letters!   Write x 1   Write x 2

1. __e__r   _____   _____
2. c__o__o__i__e   _____   _____
3. __l__p__a__t   _____   _____
4. g__r__f__e   _____   _____
5. __a__g__r__o   _____   _____
6. l__o__   _____   _____
7. __o__k__y   _____   _____
8. p__n__u__n   _____   _____
9. __h__n__   _____   _____
10. t__g__r   _____   _____

Where is the <u>monkey</u>?

✓ **The** monkey **is <u>next to</u> the <u>crocodile</u>.**

Where are the <u>elephants</u>?

✓ **The** elephants **are <u>across from</u> the <u>giraffe</u>s.**

⭐ **Winner's Tip!** Learn: next to, across from, between, near

Part 2B: Fill in the blanks

1. where _____ the _____?
   The tigers are _____ the lions and the _____.

2. _____ is _____ kangaroo?
   The _____ is _____ the _____.

3. where _____ _____ _____?
   The giraffe _____ _____ the _____.

4. _____ are _____ _____?
   The rhinos _____ _____ _____ _____.

Is the <u>bear</u> <u>between</u> the <u>tiger</u> and the <u>rhino</u>?

✓ **Yes, it is. It's between the** tiger **and the** rhino.

✗ **No, it isn't. It isn't between the** tiger **and the** rhino.

Are the <u>kangaroos</u> <u>near</u> the <u>penguins</u>?

✓ **Yes, they are. They're near the** penguins.

✗ **No, they aren't. They aren't near the** penguins.

 **Winner's Tip!** remember "s"!

Part 3B: Fill in the blanks

1. Are the crocodiles _____ the bear?
   Yes, they _____. They're across from the _____.

2. _____ the elephant _____ the _____?
   No, it _____. It _____ next to the _____.

3. Is _____ monkey _____ the lion and the _____?
   No, it isn't. It isn't _____ the _____ and the rhino.

4. Are _____ penguins _____ the crocodile?
   Yes, _____ are. _____ near _____ crocodile.

like / likes – liked – liking – liked (любити)

Every spring, they <u>like</u> going to the zoo.

He always <u>likes</u> seeing the lions and tigers.

Last time, we <u>liked</u> the giraffes the best.

She is <u>liking</u> her new job at the zoo.

I have never <u>liked</u> crocodiles very much.

Part 4B: Verb Practice

1. Every morning, I _____ eating apples and oranges.

2. On weekends, she _____ spending time with family.

3. Most days, he _____ playing with his many toys.

4. Last week, they _____ the grapes we gave them.

5. Yesterday, I _____ the pencil I saw at the store.

6. This morning, he _____ the color of the sky.

7. Right now, she is _____ the nearby fruit market.

8. They are _____ the food and drinks at the party.

9. He has never _____ the color yellow in his room.

10. We have _____ many kinds of tea before.

Part 5A: Phonics Practice

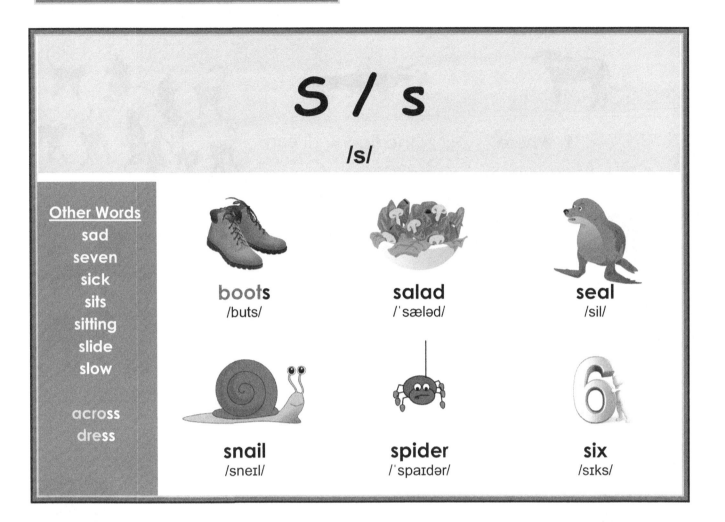

S / s

/s/

Other Words

sad
seven
sick
sits
sitting
slide
slow

across
dress

boots
/buts/

salad
/ˈsæləd/

seal
/sil/

snail
/sneɪl/

spider
/ˈspaɪdər/

six
/sɪks/

Part 5B: Write and read

1. __even __ad __eals mi__s __itting on ice.

2. __ix __low __nails __lide acro__s __alad.

3. A __ick __pider __it__ in boot__ and a dre__s.

"Is" or "are"? Answer the questions

1. Where ___is___ the tiger?   [near]

   The tiger is near the bear.

2. Where _____ the monkeys?   [between]

   _____

3. Where _____ the rhino?   [across from]

   _____

4. Where _____ the kangaroos?   [between]

   _____

5. Where _____ the penguins?   [next to]

   _____

6. Where _____ the bear?   [across from]

   _____

Lesson 12

Clothes

одяг

Part 1A: Learn the words

1. **T-shirt**
   футболка
2. **blouse**
   блузка
3. **scarf**
   Шарф
4. **coat**
   пальто
5. **dress**
   плаття

6. **hat**
   капелюх
7. **sweater**
   светр
8. **jacket**
   куртка
9. **skirt**
   спідниця
10. **necktie**
    краватка

 Practice speaking: "Шарф" is "<u>scarf</u>" in English!

Part 1B: Write the words

Write the missing letters!   Write x 1   Write x 2

1. b__o__s__   _____   _____
2. __o__t   _____   _____
3. d__e__s   _____   _____
4. __a__   _____   _____
5. j__c__e__   _____   _____
6. __e__k__i__   _____   _____
7. s__a__f   _____   _____
8. __k__r__   _____   _____
9. s__e__t__r   _____   _____
10. __-s__i__t   _____   _____

What are you wearing?

✓ **I'm wearing a <u>hat</u>. I'm not wearing a <u>scarf</u>.**

What is he wearing?

✓ **He's wearing a <u>coat</u>. He isn't wearing a <u>T-shirt</u>.**

⭐ **Winner's Tip!** I'm = I am / he's = he is / she's = she is / you're = you are / we're = we are / they're = they are

Part 2B: Fill in the blanks

1. What _____ you _____?
   I'm wearing a _____. I'm _____ _____ a hat.

2. _____ is _____ wearing?
   He's _____ a coat. _____ isn't wearing a _____.

3. What _____ _____ _____?
   She's _____ a blouse. She _____ _____ a dress.

4. _____ are _____ _____?
   _____ wearing a _____. I'm not _____ a scarf.

Are you wearing a <u>dress</u>?

✓ **Yes, I am. I'm wearing a** dress.

✗ **No, I'm not. I'm not wearing a** dress.

Is she wearing a <u>jacket</u>?

✓ **Yes, she is. She's wearing a** jacket.

✗ **No, she isn't. She isn't wearing a** jacket.

 **Winner's Tip!** remember "a"!

Part 3B: Fill in the blanks

1. Is _____ wearing a _____?
   Yes, he _____. _____ wearing _____ T-shirt.

2. Are _____ _____ a sweater?
   No, _____ not. _____ not _____ a sweater.

3. _____ she _____ a necktie?
   No, _____ _____. _____ isn't wearing a necktie.

4. Are _____ _____ a _____?
   Yes, I _____. _____ wearing _____ jacket.

wear / wears – wore – wearing – worn (ностит)

On cold days, I **wear** a very warm jacket.

Sometimes, she **wears** her new blouse.

Yesterday, they **wore** green sweaters.

He is **wearing** a T-shirt and a hat right now.

She has never **worn** a skirt to school.

Part 4B: Verb Practice

1. Every winter, I _____ my warmest coat and scarf.
2. On Saturdays, she _____ her favorite clothes.
3. Every Sunday, he _____ a jacket for his job.
4. Last month, they _____ yellow scarves at school.
5. Last Monday, I _____ my old ugly jacket outside.
6. Yesterday, she _____ a blue T-shirt and a red skirt.
7. Right now, he is _____ an expensive black sweater.
8. I'm _____ a long gray necktie right now.
9. He has never _____ the coat that I gave to him.
10. You have _____ that purple T-shirt many times.

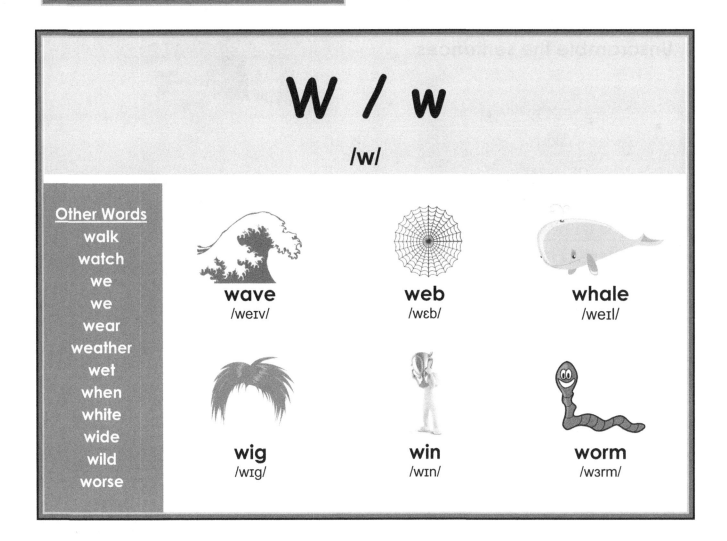

W / w

/w/

Other Words
walk
watch
we
we
wear
weather
wet
when
white
wide
wild
worse

wave
/weɪv/

web
/wɛb/

whale
/weɪl/

wig
/wɪg/

win
/wɪn/

worm
/wɜrm/

1. __e __atch __et __hales __ear __igs.

2. __eather is __orse __hen __hite __orms __in.

3. __alk __ide of __ebs and __ild __aves.

Unscramble the sentences

she wearing a skirt is Yes She's

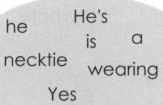

1. <u>Yes, she is. She's wearing a skirt.</u>

coat wearing wearing a He a He's hat isn't

2. _____
_____

he He's is a necktie wearing Yes

3. _____

blouse scarf a isn't She wearing a wearing She's

4. _____
_____

T-shirt isn't No She she wearing isn't a

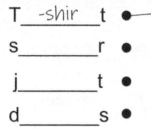

5. _____

Complete the words and match

T___-shir___t •

s_____r •

j_____t •

d_____s •

Lesson 13 Countries

країни

Part 1A: Learn the words

1. **Japan**
   Японія
2. **Canada**
   Канада
3. **Brazil**
   Бразилія
4. **Australia**
   Австралія
5. **South Africa**
   Південна Африка

6. **China**
   Китай
7. **Mexico**
   Мексика
8. **Argentina**
   Аргентина
9. **New Zealand**
   Нова Зеландія
10. **Kenya**
    Кенія

 Practice speaking: "Південна Африка " means "<u>South Africa</u>"!

Part 1B: Write the words

Write the missing letters!   Write x 1   Write x 2

1. A_g_n_i_a _____ _____
2. _u_t_a_i_ _____ _____
3. B_a_i_ _____ _____
4. _a_a_a _____ _____
5. C_i_a _____ _____
6. _a_a_ _____ _____
7. K_n_a _____ _____
8. _e_i_o _____ _____
9. N_w _e_l_n_ _____ _____
10. _o_t_ A_r_c__ _____ _____

Where are you going?

✓ **We're going to <u>Australia</u>. We're not going to <u>China</u>.**

Where's she going?

✓ **She's going to <u>Brazil</u>. She isn't going to <u>Kenya</u>.**

 **Winner's Tip!** where's = where is

Part 2B: Fill in the blanks

1. Where _____ you _____?
   I'm _____ to _____. I'm not going to Canada.

2. _____ are _____ going?
   They're going to _____. They _____ going to Mexico.

3. Where's _____ _____?
   She's _____ to _____. She _____ going to China.

4. _____ _____ _____?
   He's going to _____. He _____ _____ to Japan.

Are they going to <u>Canada</u>?

✓ **Yes, they are. They're going to Canada.**
✗ **No, they're not. They're not going to Canada.**

Is he going to <u>Mexico</u>?

✓ **Yes, he is. He's going to Mexico.**
✗ **No, he isn't. He isn't going to Mexico.**

 Winner's Tip! He isn't = He's not, etc.

Part 3B: Fill in the blanks

1. _____ you _____ to New Zealand?
   Yes, I _____. I'm _____ to _____.

2. _____ she _____ to _____?
   No, _____ isn't. She _____ going to Argentina.

3. Is _____ _____ to _____?
   No, he isn't. _____ isn't _____ to South Africa.

4. Are _____ _____ _____ Brazil?
   Yes, we _____. We're _____ _____ Brazil.

write / writes – wrote – writing – written (писати)

Every evening, I <u>write</u> things in my journal.

She usually <u>writes</u> stories to tell her niece.

Last year, he <u>wrote</u> a book about travel.

We are <u>writing</u> about our feelings right now.

They have never <u>written</u> any English words.

Part 4B: Verb Practice

1. Every afternoon, I _____ down my ideas for dinner.
2. On Thursdays, she _____ on paper at her desk.
3. Every week, he _____ about different countries.
4. Last class, we _____ homework about Australia.
5. Last week, I _____ a letter to my friend in Japan.
6. Earlier today, we _____ down some ideas on Canada.
7. Right now, she is _____ to her family in Argentina.
8. We are _____ in the English class right now.
9. He has never _____ any good stories before.
10. We have _____ down a lot of information already.

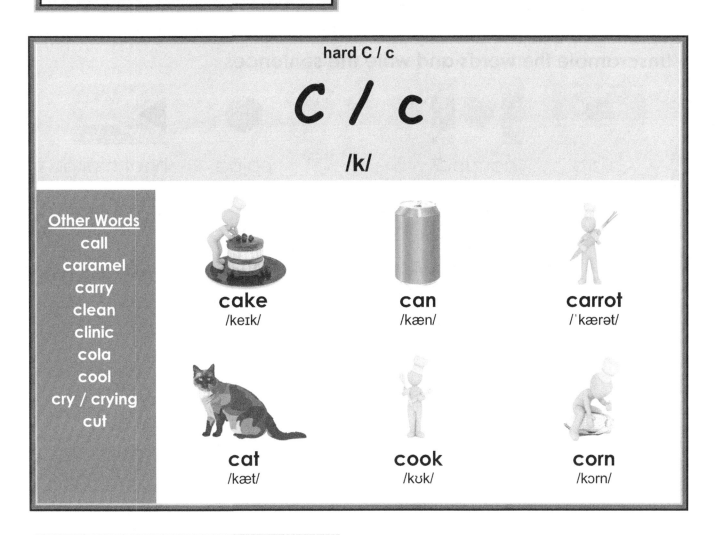

hard C / c

C / c

/k/

Other Words
call
caramel
carry
clean
clinic
cola
cool
cry / crying
cut

cake
/keɪk/

can
/kæn/

carrot
/ˈkærət/

cat
/kæt/

cook
/kʊk/

corn
/kɔrn/

Part 5B: Write and read

1. __ool __ooks __ut __aramel __ake.

2. __rying __ats __an __all __lean __lini__s.

3. __arry __orn, __arrots and __ola __ans.

Unscramble the words and write the sentences

alizrb   aandac
Brazil   _Canada_

najpa   shuot cfaira
_____   _____

1. He _'s going to Brazil._
    He isn't going to Canada.

2. They _____
    _____

3.   yaekn
_____

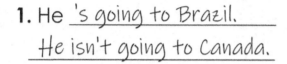

4.   etganrian
_____

coiexm   iulrstaaa
_____   _____

niahc   ewn aaelnzd
_____   _____

5. We _____
_____

6. She _____
_____

Lesson 14 Places

місця

Part 1A: Learn the words

1. **park**
   парк
2. **beach**
   пляж
3. **night market**
   нічний ринок
4. **store**
   магазин
5. **supermarket**
   супермаркет

6. **restaurant**
   ресторан
7. **swimming pool**
   басейн
8. **department store**
   універмаг
9. **cinema**
   кінотеатр
10. **gym**
    спортзал

 Practice speaking: "пляж " means "<u>beach</u>"!

Part 1B: Write the words

Write the missing letters!   Write x 1   Write x 2

1. b__a__h   _____   _____
2. __i__e__a   _____   _____
3. d__p__rtm__nt st__re   _____   _____
4. __y__   _____   _____
5. n__g__t __a__k__t   _____   _____
6. p__r__   _____   _____
7. __e__t__u__a__t   _____   _____
8. s__o__e   _____   _____
9. __u__e__m__r__e__   _____   _____
10. s__i__m__n__ p__ol   _____   _____

Who are you going to the <u>restaurant</u> with?

✓ I'm going to the restaurant with my <u>brother</u>.
✗ I'm not going to the restaurant with my <u>sister</u>.

Who's she going to the <u>beach</u> with?

✓ She's going to the beach with her <u>cousin</u>.
✗ She's not going to the beach with her <u>uncle</u>.

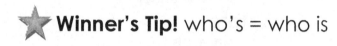 **Winner's Tip!** who's = who is

Part 2B: Fill in the blanks

1. _____ are _____ going to the _____ with?
   I'm _____ to the park _____ my _____.

2. who's he _____ to the cinema _____?
   _____ not going to the _____ with _____ sister.

3. _____ are _____ going to the restaurant with?
   They're _____ to the _____ with his _____.

4. _____ she _____ to _____ gym _____?
   _____ going _____ the _____ with her brother.

84

Are we going to the <u>store</u> with my <u>aunt</u>?

✓ **Yes, we are. We're going to the** store **with** her**.**
✗ **No, we're not. We're not going there with your** aunt**.**

Is she going to the <u>gym</u> with your <u>father</u>?

✓ **Yes, she is. She's going to the** gym **with my** father**.**
✗ **No, she isn't. She isn't going there with** him**.**

 Winner's Tip! my, your, his, her, its, our, their

Part 3B: Fill in the blanks

1. Are you _____ to the store _____ your uncle?
   No, I'm not. I'm _____ going _____ with him.

2. Is _____ going to the park with your _____?
   No, he _____. He isn't _____ there with her.

3. _____ we going to the gym _____ my aunt?
   No, we _____. We aren't _____ there with her.

4. Is _____ going to the store with her _____?
   Yes, _____ is. She's _____ _____ with him.

Part 4A: Verb of the day

walk / walks – walked – walking – walked (ходити, гуляти)

Every morning, we <u>walk</u> to school together.

He usually <u>walks</u> in the park each afternoon.

Yesterday, they <u>walked</u> home from the store.

She is <u>walking</u> to the gym with him right now.

I have never <u>walked</u> very far at the beach.

Part 4B: Verb Practice

1. Every evening, they _____ around the night market.
2. On Tuesdays, she _____ to the department store.
3. Every weekend, he _____ to the swimming pool.
4. Yesterday, we _____ home from the supermarket.
5. Last weekend, I _____ to many different places.
6. Last night, she _____ for a long time at the park.
7. Right now, he is _____ from the store to the gym.
8. I am _____ at the zoo right now with my friend.
9. He has never _____ very much in his life.
10. You have _____ to almost every place in this city.

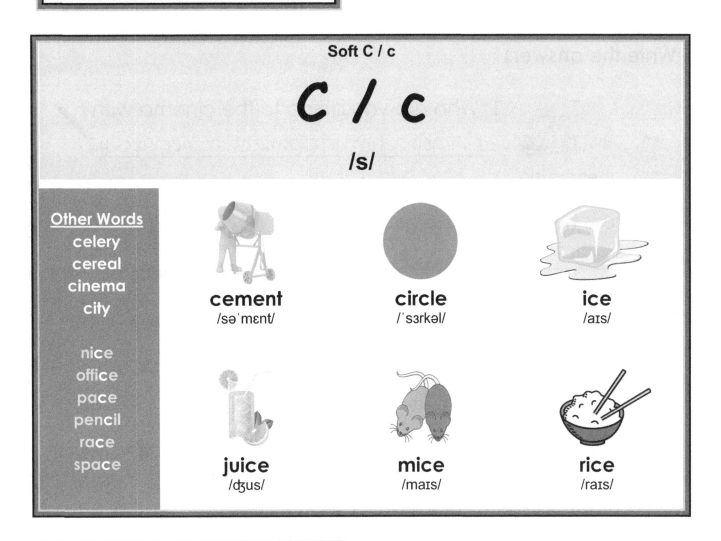

Soft C / c

C / c

/s/

Other Words

celery
cereal
cinema
city

nice
office
pace
pencil
race
space

cement
/səˈmɛnt/

circle
/ˈsɜrkəl/

ice
/aɪs/

juice
/dʒus/

mice
/maɪs/

rice
/raɪs/

Part 5B: Write and read

1. __inema mi__e ra__e __ircles pa__ing i__e.

2. Jui__e, ri__e, __elery and __ereal taste ni__e.

3. __ement __ity offi__e spa__e sells pen__ils.

Part 6: Fun review

Write the answers

  1. Who are you going to the cinema with?
<u>I'm going to the cinema with her cousin.</u>

her cousin

2. Who is he going to the gym with?

_____ my brother

  **3.** Who is she going to the restaurant with?

_____

your sister

4. Who are they going to the park with?

_____ his niece

Write the questions

 1. <u>Are you going to the swimming pool with his aunt?</u>

Yes, I am. I'm going to the swimming pool with his aunt.

 2. _____

No, he isn't. He's not going to the store with my grandfather.

 3. _____

Yes, we are. We're going to the park with her father.

Lesson 15 Transportation

транспорт

Part 1A: Learn the words

1. take an **airplane**
   летіти літаком
2. ride a **bicycle**
   їздити на велосипеді
3. catch a **bus**
   сідати на автобус
4. drive a **car**
   водити машину
5. take a **ferry**
   переправлятися на поромі

6. ride a **motorcycle**
   їздити на мотоциклі
7. ride a **scooter**
   їздити на скутері
8. take the **subway**
   їздити на метро
9. take a **taxi**
   брати таксі
10. take a **train**
    їздити потягом

 Practice speaking: "їздити потягом" means "_take a train_"!

Part 1B: Write the words

Write the missing letters!   Write x 1   Write x 2

1. __i__p__a__e   _____   _____
2. b__c__c__e   _____   _____
3. __u__   _____   _____
4. __a__   _____   _____
5. f__r__y   _____   _____
6. __o__o__c__c__e   _____   _____
7. s__o__t__r   _____   _____
8. __u__w__y   _____   _____
9. t__x__   _____   _____
10. __r__i__   _____   _____

How do you get to the <u>department store</u>?

✓ I **<u>catch a bus</u>** to get to the department store.
✗ I don't **<u>take a taxi</u>** to get there.

How does he get to the <u>beach</u>?

✓ He **<u>takes an airplane</u>** to get to the beach.
✗ He **doesn't <u>take a ferry</u>** to get there.

 Winner's Tip! Answer with "there" for the <u>place</u>

Part 2B: Fill in the blanks

1. _____ do you _____ to the _____?
   I _____ to get _____ the beach.

2. How _____ he get to _____ restaurant?
   He doesn't _____ to _____ there.

3. How _____ she _____ to the _____?
   She _____ to _____ _____ the gym.

4. _____ do _____ get to the _____?
   They _____ to _____ to _____ store.

Part 3A: Yes / No questions

Do you <u>ride a scooter</u> to get to the <u>swimming pool</u>?

✓ **Yes, I do. I** ride a scooter **to get** there.

✗ **No, I don't. I don't** ride a scooter **to get** there.

Does he <u>take the subway</u> to get to the <u>cinema</u>?

✓ **Yes, he does. He** takes the subway **to get** there.

✗ **No, he doesn't. He doesn't** take the subway **to get** there.

 Winner's Tip! Remember: he / she / it verb + s

Part 3B: Fill in the blanks

1. Do _____ _____ to get to _____ park?
   Yes, I do. I ride a bicycle to _____ to the _____.

2. Does he _____ to _____ to the beach?
   No, he _____. He _____ take a taxi to get there.

3. Do _____ _____ to get to the swimming pool?
   Yes, we _____. We take the subway to get _____.

4. Does she _____ to _____ to the store?
   Yes, she _____. She _____ to get _____.

visit / visits – visited – visiting – visited (відвідувати)

Every year, you <u>visit</u> your family in Paris.

He usually <u>visits</u> us in the late afternoon.

Yesterday, I <u>visited</u> her at the beach.

They are <u>visiting</u> from Europe right now.

We have never <u>visited</u> another country.

Part 4B: Verb Practice

1. Every summer, I _____ my family living in America.

2. On weekends, she _____ her sick grandmother.

3. Every Sunday, he _____ the library and reads books.

4. Last winter, they _____ Europe and went skiing.

5. Last weekend, I _____ my friend in the hospital.

6. Last spring, we _____ an amazing national park.

7. Right now, he is _____ his cousins in the city.

8. We are _____ with my aunt and uncle right now.

9. She has never _____ Asia or Australia before.

10. I have _____ many incredible countries so far.

ou / ow

/aʊ/

Other Words
count
found
loud
round
shout
sound
crowd
down
frown
how
now
town

cloud
/klaʊd/

house
/haʊs/

mouse
/maʊs/

clown
/klaʊn/

cow
/kaʊ/

owl
/aʊl/

Part 5B: Write and read

1. D___n cl___ns f___nd h___ c___s fr___n.

2. N___ r___nd ___ls c___nt l___d cr___ds.

3. T___n h___se m___se sh___ts cl___d s___nds.

Part 6: Fun review

Catch, drive, ride, or take? Choose a place, write sentences

drive	She _drives a car to get to the beach._
_____	We _____
_____	They _____
_____	You _____
_____	He _____
_____	I _____

Write questions

_____	_Does_ she _take a train to get_ _to Mexico?_
_____	_____ he _____ _____
_____	_____ you _____ _____
_____	_____ we _____ _____

Winner's Tip - Places: park, beach, night market, store, supermarket, restaurant, swimming pool, department store, cinema, gym, (country names)

Write the correct answer next to the letter "A"

A: ___ **1.** Where _____ the penguins? The penguins are _____ the lion.
a) is / next to   **b)** are / between
c) is / across from   **d)** are / near

A: ___ **2.** What are you _____? I'm not _____ a hat.
a) wearing / wear   **b)** wearing / wearing
c) wore / wear   **d)** wears / worn

A: ___ **3.** _____ she going? She's _____ to Japan.
a) Where / gone   **b)** Where are / go
c) Where's / going   **d)** Where is / went

A: ___ **4.** _____ are all _____ to the supermarket right now.
a) We / walk   **b)** They / walking
c) You / walked   **d)** They're / walking

A: ___ **5.** How do you _____ to the restaurant? I take a taxi to get _____.
a) get / there   **b)** go / restaurant
c) go / to restaurant   **d)** getting / to there

A: ___ **6.** Do you _____ an airplane to _____ your family?
a) ride / visit   **b)** take / visited
c) catch / visiting   **d)** take / visit

A: ___ **7.** He usually _____ to the cinema after _____ work.
a) walks / his   **b)** walking / he
c) walk / done   **d)** walked / did

A: ___ **8.** Are we _____ to Kenya? Yes, we are. _____ going to Kenya.
a) going / We're   **b)** go / We are
c) going / We've   **d)** gone / We

A: ___ **9.** Is he _____ a T-shirt? Yes, he is. _____ wearing a T-shirt.
a) wear / He is   **b)** wears / He
c) wearing / He's   **d)** worn / He has

A: ___ **10.** Is the rhino _____ the bear? No, it _____. It isn't next to the bear.
a) near / don't
b) between / doesn't
c) across from / not
d) next to / isn't

A: ___ **11.** My mother _____ a letter to her friend in China last _____.
a) wrote / month
b) writes / week
c) write / year
d) writing / time

A: ___ **12.** I usually _____ a bicycle to _____ my friend at the beach.
a) take / visiting
b) ride / visit
c) catch / visited
d) ride / visits

A: ___ **13.** _____ always _____ the giraffes at the zoo.
a) They / like
b) We / likes
c) You / liking
d) She / like

A: ___ **14.** Who are you _____ to the swimming pool with?
I'm going to the swimming pool _____ my uncle.
a) going / by
b) go / for
c) going / with
d) goes / to

A: ___ **15.** He _____ never _____ a necktie to the office.
a) is / wear
b) have / wore
c) has / worn
d) has / wearing

A: ___ **16.** Where _____ they going? _____ going to China.
a) is / They
b) 're / They are
c) have / They've
d) are / They're

A: ___ **17.** I _____ never _____ monkeys very much.
a) am / liking
b) have / liked
c) have / likes
d) am / liked

A: ___ **18.** Is she going to the store with your nephew? Yes, she is. She's
going _____ with _____.
a) to store / nephew
b) there / him
c) in / her
d) there / her

Answers on page 257

Lesson 16   Meats

м'ясо

Part 1A: Learn the words

1. **beef**
   яловичина
2. **pork**
   свинина
3. **bacon**
   бекон
4. **fish**
   риба
5. **salami**
   салямі

6. **chicken**
   курятина
7. **lamb**
   баранина
8. **ham**
   шинка
9. **sausage**
   ковбаса
10. **shrimp**
    креветки

 Practice speaking: "курятина " is "_chicken_" in English!

Part 1B: Write the words

Write the missing letters!   Write x 1   Write x 2

1. b__c__n
2. __e__f
3. c__i__k__n
4. __i__h
5. __a__
6. l__m__
7. __o__k
8. s__l__m__
9. __a__s__g__
10. s__r__m__

97

What kind of meat did you eat for <u>dinner</u>?

✓ **We ate <u>shrimp</u> for dinner. We didn't eat <u>ham</u>.**

What kind of meat did he eat for <u>lunch</u>?

✓ **He ate <u>beef</u> for lunch. He didn't eat <u>fish</u>.**

 Winner's Tip! Learn: breakfast, lunch, dinner, a snack

Part 2B: Fill in the blanks

1. What _____ of _____ did you _____ for lunch?
   I _____ ham. I _____ eat _____.

2. What _____ of _____ did she _____ for dinner?
   _____ _____ pork. She _____ eat lamb.

3. _____ kind of meat _____ he eat for _____?
   He ate _____. He _____ _____ salami.

4. _____ kind of meat _____ they eat for _____?
   They _____ beef. _____ _____ _____ shrimp.

Part 3A: Yes / No questions

Did you eat <u>sausage</u> for <u>breakfast</u>?

✓ **Yes, I did. I ate** sausage **for breakfast.**

✗ **No, I didn't. I didn't eat** sausage **for breakfast.**

Did she eat <u>chicken</u> for <u>a snack</u>?

✓ **Yes, she did. She ate** chicken **for a snack.**

✗ **No, she didn't. She didn't eat** chicken **for a snack.**

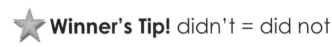 **Winner's Tip!** didn't = did not

Part 3B: Fill in the blanks

1. _____ you eat _____ for lunch?
   Yes, I _____. I _____ lamb for _____.

2. Did _____ eat _____ for _____?
   No, she _____. She _____ eat pork for a snack.

3. Did _____ _____ bacon for _____?
   No, they _____. They _____ eat bacon for lunch.

4. Did _____ _____ _____ for _____?
   Yes, he did. He _____ _____ for _____.

Part 4A: Verb of the day

eat / eats – ate – eating – eaten (їсти)

Every morning, we _eat_ bacon for breakfast.

Sometimes, she _eats_ too much meat.

Yesterday, they _ate_ lunch with my family.

He is _eating_ a pizza with his brother now.

We have never _eaten_ food from Japan.

Part 4B: Verb Practice

1. Daily, she _____ many different vegetables.
2. On Thursdays, we _____ at a restaurant nearby.
3. Every Tuesday, he _____ with me at the park.
4. Last week, he _____ some great Ukrainian food.
5. Yesterday, I _____ a delicious cake with my friend.
6. Last time, we _____ some grapes and cherries.
7. Right now, she is _____ some tasty apple pie.
8. They are _____ many kinds of meat right now.
9. He has never _____ shrimp or fish before.
10. I have _____ many kinds of fruits this week.

Part 5A: Phonics Practice

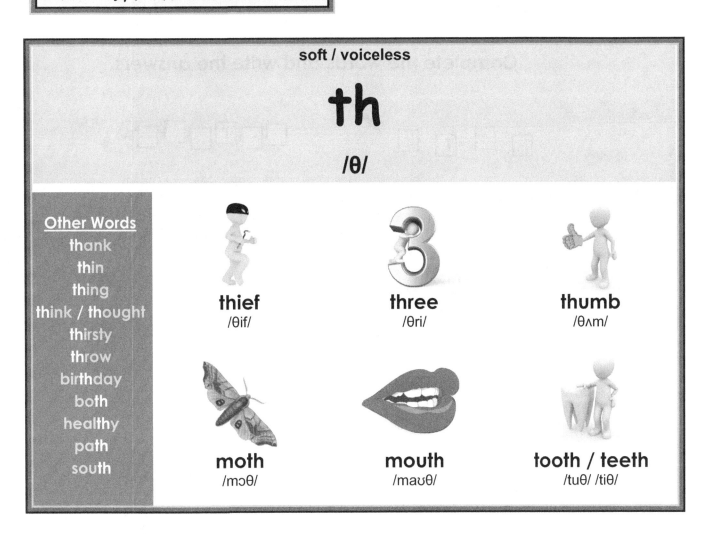

soft / voiceless

th

/θ/

Other Words
thank
thin
thing
think / thought
thirsty
throw
birthday
both
healthy
path
south

thief
/θif/

three
/θri/

thumb
/θʌm/

moth
/mɔθ/

mouth
/maʊθ/

tooth / teeth
/tuθ/ /tiθ/

Part 5B: Write and read

1. A heal___y ___in ___ief ___rows ___ree ___ings.

2. A ___irsty mo___ mou___ ___anks tee___.

3. Bo___ bir___day ___umbs ___ink sou___ pa___.

Part 6: Fun review

Complete the words and write the answers

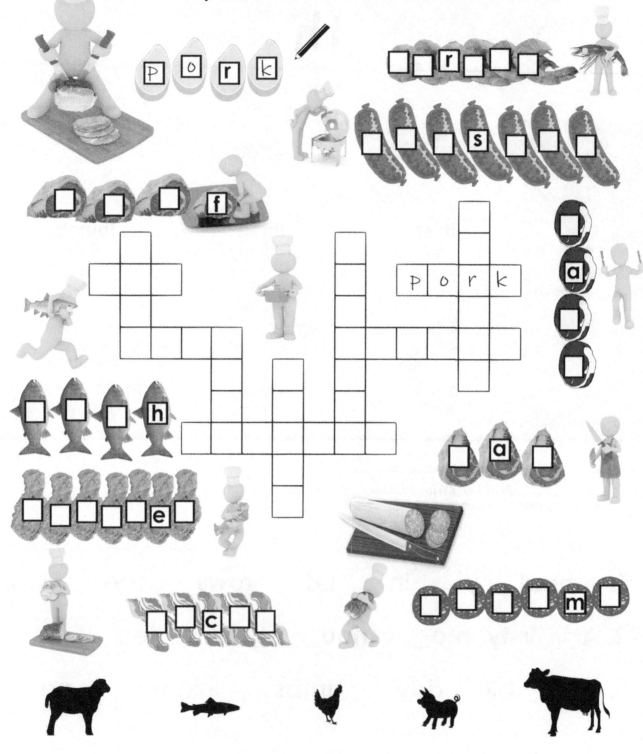

102

Lesson 17 — At school

в школі

Part 1A: Learn the words

1. **classroom**
   класна кімната
2. **office**
   кабінет
3. **nurse's office**
   кабінет медсестри
4. **gym**
   спортзал
5. **hall**
   вестибюль

6. **computer lab**
   комп'ютерний клас
7. **art room**
   художній зал
8. **music room**
   музичний клас
9. **science lab**
   наукова лабораторія
10. **lunchroom**
    їдальня

 Practice speaking: "їдальня " is "_lunchroom_" in English!

Part 1B: Write the words

Write the missing letters!   Write x 1   Write x 2

1. __r__ r_o__   _____   _____
2. c__a_s_o_m   _____   _____
3. __o_p_t_r l_b   _____   _____
4. __y__   _____   _____
5. h_l__   _____   _____
6. __u__c_r_o__   _____   _____
7. m__s_c __o_m   _____   _____
8. __u_s__'s __f_i_e   _____   _____
9. o_f_c__   _____   _____
10. __c_e_c__ l_b   _____   _____

Where did you see the <u>teacher</u> <u>yesterday</u>?

✓ Yesterday, **I saw the** teacher **in the** <u>office</u>.

✗ Yesterday, **I didn't see the** teacher **in the** <u>hall</u>.

Where did she see the <u>principal</u> <u>last week</u>?

✓ Last week, **she saw the** principal **in the** <u>science lab</u>.

✗ Last week, **she didn't see the** principal **in the** <u>art room</u>.

 Winner's Tip! Learn: yesterday, last week, last month

Part 2B: Fill in the blanks

1. where _____ he _____ the teacher _____?
   Last week, he _____ the teacher in the_____.

2. where _____ she _____ the principal _____?
   Yesterday, she _____ see the _____ in the hall.

3. _____ did _____ see the _____ last month?
   _____, I saw the coach _____ the _____.

4. _____ _____ he see the _____ yesterday?
   Yesterday, he _____ see the _____ in the _____.

Did he see a <u>classmate</u> in the <u>art room</u> <u>last week</u>?

✓ **Yes, he did. He saw a** classmate there last week.
✗ **No, he didn't. He didn't see a** classmate there last week.

Did they see a <u>coach</u> in the <u>gym</u> <u>yesterday</u>?

✓ **Yes, they did. They saw a** coach there yesterday.
✗ **No, they didn't. They didn't see a** coach there yesterday.

 Winner's Tip! Learn: teacher, principal, coach, classmate

Part 3B: Fill in the blanks

1. Did you see a _____ in the gym _____?
   Yes, I _____. I _____ a teacher there yesterday.

2. _____ she see a _____ in the office _____?
   Yes, she did. She _____ a coach there last week.

3. Did he _____ a classmate in the hall _____?
   No, he didn't. He didn't see a _____ there last month.

4. Did we see a _____ in the _____ _____?
   Yes, _____ did. We saw a _____ there _____.

put / puts – put – putting – put (ставити)

Every day, I <u>put</u> my books in the office.

He usually <u>puts</u> pencils in the art room.

Yesterday, he <u>put</u> some balls in the gym.

She is <u>putting</u> chairs in the music room.

He has never <u>put</u> anything in the hall.

Part 4B: Verb Practice

1. Each day, he _____ some papers in the office.

2. On Fridays, she _____ some fruit in the lunchroom.

3. Every Monday, I _____ a blue T-shirt in my bag.

4. Yesterday, he _____ some milk in his coffee.

5. Last time, we _____ more cheese on our pizza.

6. Last week, she _____ some books on the bookshelf.

7. Right now, she is _____ some drinks in the car.

8. They are _____ some toys with the monkeys.

9. I have never _____ fruit into a salad before.

10. He has _____ meat in his lunches for many years.

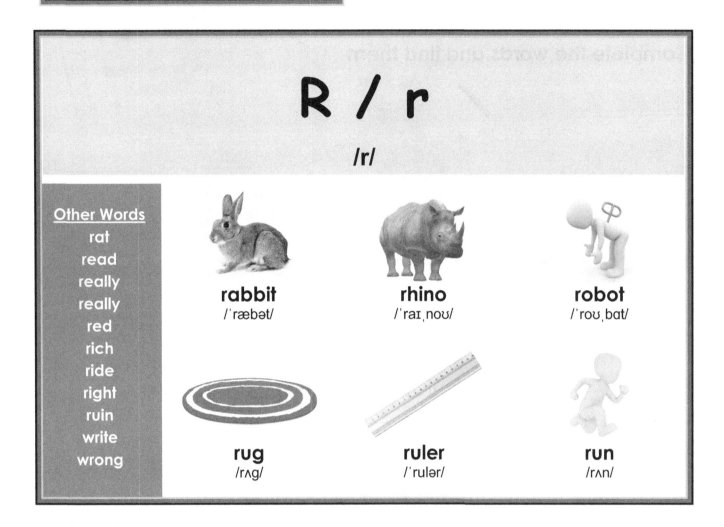

R / r

/r/

Other Words
rat
read
really
really
red
rich
ride
right
ruin
write
wrong

rabbit
/ˈræbət/

rhino
/ˈraɪˌnoʊ/

robot
/ˈroʊˌbɑt/

rug
/rʌg/

ruler
/ˈrulər/

run
/rʌn/

Part 5B: Write and read

1. __ed __abbits __ide __obot __hinos __ight.

2. W__ong __ulers __eally __uin __ugs.

3. __eally __ich __ats __ead, __un and w__ite.

Complete the words and find them

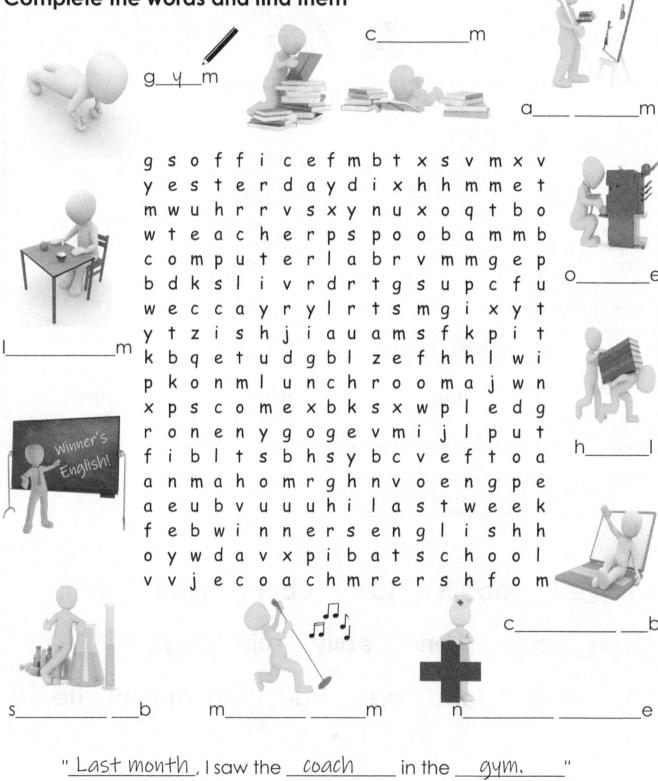

c_____m

g__y__m

a____ _____m

g	s	o	f	f	i	c	e	f	m	b	t	x	s	v	m	x	v
y	e	s	t	e	r	d	a	y	d	i	x	h	h	m	m	e	t
m	w	u	h	r	r	v	s	x	y	n	u	x	o	q	t	b	o
w	t	e	a	c	h	e	r	p	s	p	o	o	b	a	m	m	b
c	o	m	p	u	t	e	r	l	a	b	r	v	m	m	g	e	p
b	d	k	s	l	i	v	r	d	r	t	g	s	u	p	c	f	u
w	e	c	c	a	y	r	y	l	r	t	s	m	g	i	x	y	t
y	t	z	i	s	h	j	i	a	u	a	m	s	f	k	p	i	t
k	b	q	e	t	u	d	g	b	l	z	e	f	h	h	l	w	i
p	k	o	n	m	l	u	n	c	h	r	o	o	m	a	j	w	n
x	p	s	c	o	m	e	x	b	k	s	x	w	p	l	e	d	g
r	o	n	e	n	y	g	o	g	e	v	m	i	j	l	p	u	t
f	i	b	l	t	s	b	h	s	y	b	c	v	e	f	t	o	a
a	n	m	a	h	o	m	r	g	h	n	v	o	e	n	g	p	e
a	e	u	b	v	u	u	u	h	i	l	a	s	t	w	e	e	k
f	e	b	w	i	n	n	e	r	s	e	n	g	l	i	s	h	h
o	y	w	d	a	v	x	p	i	b	a	t	s	c	h	o	o	l
v	v	j	e	c	o	a	c	h	m	r	e	r	s	h	f	o	m

o_____e

l_____m

Winner's English!

h_____l

c_____b

s_____b

m_____m

n_____e

" __Last month__ , I saw the ___coach___ in the ___gym.___ "

Lesson 18 More clothes

додатковий одяг

Part 1A: Learn the words

1. **pants**
   штани
2. **shorts**
   шорти
3. **shoes**
   взуття
4. **dresses**
   сукні
5. **shirts**
   сорочки

6. **jeans**
   джинси
7. **socks**
   шкарпетки
8. **gloves**
   рукавички
9. **pajamas**
   піжами
10. **boots**
    черевики

 Practice speaking: "взуття " is "<u>shoes</u>" in English!

Part 1B: Write the words

Write the missing letters!   Write x 1   Write x 2

1. __o__t__   _____   _____
2. d__e__s__s   _____   _____
3. __l__v__s   _____   _____
4. j__a__s   _____   _____
5. __a__a__a__   _____   _____
6. p__n__s   _____   _____
7. __h__r__s   _____   _____
8. s__o__s   _____   _____
9. __h__r__s   _____   _____
10. s__c__s   _____   _____

Part 2A: Ask a question

Where did you buy these <u>gloves</u>?

✓ **I bought these** gloves <u>at the department store</u>.

✗ **I didn't buy** them <u>at the shopping mall</u>.

Where did she buy those <u>dresses</u>?

✓ **She bought those** dresses <u>online</u>.

✗ **She didn't buy** them <u>at the store</u>.

 Winner's Tip! Learn: online

Part 2B: Fill in the blanks

1. Where _____ he _____ those pajamas?

   He _____ those _____ at the department store.

2. _____ _____ she buy these _____?

   _____ bought _____ dresses online.

3. _____ _____ you buy those _____?

   I _____ buy _____ at the store.

4. _____ _____ they _____ those _____?

   _____ didn't _____ _____ online.

Did he buy these <u>pants</u> in <u>Japan</u>?

✓ **Yes, he did. He bought these** pants **in** Japan.

✗ **No, he didn't. He didn't buy** them there.

Did we buy those <u>socks</u> in <u>Canada</u>?

✓ **Yes, we did. We bought those** socks **in** Canada.

✗ **No, we didn't. We didn't buy** them there.

 Winner's Tip! Answer with "them" for plural nouns

Part 3B: Fill in the blanks

1. Did _____ buy those _____ in _____?
   Yes, she did. She _____ _____ shorts in Korea.

2. Did _____ _____ these shoes _____ China?
   No, he _____. He didn't buy them _____.

3. Did _____ buy those jeans in _____?
   No, _____ _____. They didn't _____ them there.

4. Did _____ buy _____ _____ in _____?
   Yes, I _____. I _____ _____ boots in Mexico.

lend / lends – lent – lending – lent (позичати, давати)

Every day, I <u>lend</u> money to my friend.

Sometimes, she <u>lends</u> me her bicycle.

Yesterday, he <u>lent</u> her some socks.

He is <u>lending</u> us some green pencils.

I have never <u>lent</u> anything to him.

Part 4B: Verb Practice

1. Every class, I _____ my classmate a colored pen.

2. On Thursdays, she _____ a board game to us.

3. Every week, he _____ his car to his brother.

4. Last time, they _____ him a toy dinosaur.

5. Last weekend, I _____ a book to my best friend.

6. Yesterday, we _____ some glue to her sister.

7. Right now, she is _____ us some markers and tape.

8. We are _____ him some clothes for the party.

9. She has never _____ money to her niece.

10. You have _____ many toys to people this month.

Part 5A: Phonics Practice

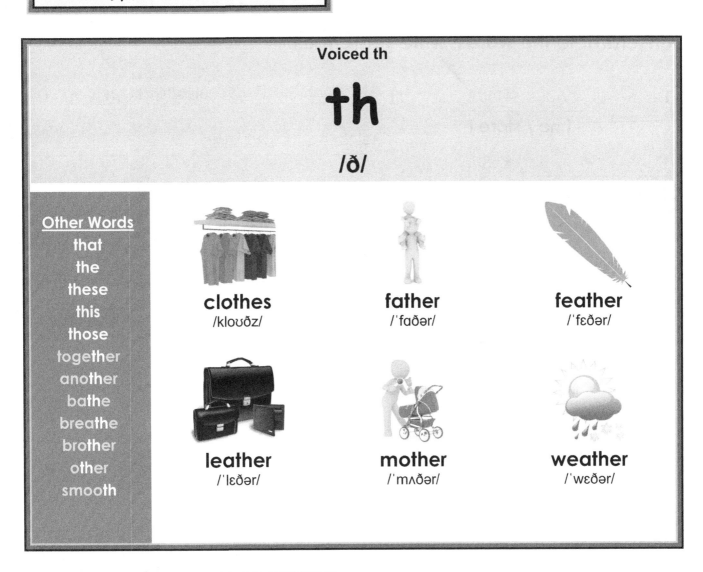

Voiced th

th

/ð/

Other Words
that
the
these
this
those
together
another
bathe
breathe
brother
other
smooth

clothes
/kloʊðz/

father
/ˈfaðər/

feather
/ˈfɛðər/

leather
/ˈlɛðər/

mother
/ˈmʌðər/

weather
/ˈwɛðər/

Part 5B: Write and read

1. Mo___er ba___es ___e o___er bro___er.

2. Brea___e ano___er fea___er toge___er.

3. Fa___er's smoo___ lea___er wea___er clo___es.

Unscramble the words, write sentences

1. H O E S S these shoes
[he / store]

2. R S H T S O
_____
[where / she]

3. I S T R S H
_____
[you / mall]

4. E S E S R S D
_____
[where / I]

1. He bought these shoes at the store.
2. Where did she buy _____ ?
3. _____
4. _____

these
those

Winner's Tip!
-"at the" <u>place</u>
-"in" <u>country name</u>
-"online"

5. _____
6. _____
7. _____
8. _____

those
[she / store]
5. n e s s j a

6. o s c s k
[where / you]

7. v o l s g e
[they / Japan]

8. s t o o b
[where / he]

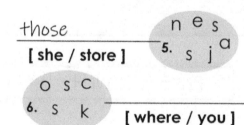

Lesson 19 More places

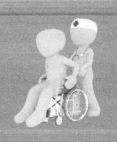

додаткові місця

Part 1A: Learn the words

1. the **bus stop**
   автобусна зупинка

2. the **clinic**
   поліклініка

3. the **factory**
   фабрика, завод

4. the **fire station**
   пожежне депо

5. the **hospital**
   лікарня

6. the **library**
   бібліотека

7. the **office**
   офіс

8. the **police station**
   міліція

9. the **school**
   школа

10. the **train station**
    залізнична станція

 Practice speaking: "бібліотека " means "<u>library</u>"!

Part 1B: Write the words

Write the missing letters!   Write x 1   Write x 2

1. b__s __t_p   _____   _____
2. __l_n__c   _____   _____
3. f__c__o__y   _____   _____
4. __i_e __t_t_o__   _____   _____
5. h__s__i__a__   _____   _____
6. __i_r_r__   _____   _____
7. o__f__c__   _____   _____
8. __o__i_e s__a__i_n   _____   _____
9. s__h__o__   _____   _____
10. __r_i__ s__a__i_n   _____   _____

Part 2A: Ask a question

Where will you go <u>tomorrow</u>?

✓ Tomorrow, I'll go to <u>the library</u>. I won't go to <u>the school</u>.

Where will he go <u>later</u>?

✓ Later, **he'll go to <u>the clinic</u>. He won't go to <u>the office</u>.**

⭐ **Winner's Tip!** won't = will not
Use: later, tomorrow, next week, next month

Part 2B: Fill in the blanks

1. Where _____ you go _____?
   Next week, I'll go to _____. I won't go to _____.

2. _____ will _____ go _____?
   Later, _____ go to _____. He won't go to the office.

3. _____ _____ she _____ _____?
   Tomorrow, she'll go to _____. She won't go to _____.

4. _____ _____ we _____ _____?
   Next month, we'll go to _____. We won't go to _____.

Will you go to <u>the police station</u> <u>next week</u>?

✓ **Yes, I will. I'll go** there next week.
✗ **No, I won't. I won't go** there next week.

Will they go to <u>the train station</u> <u>next month</u>?

✓ **Yes, they will. They'll go** there next month.
✗ **No, they won't. They won't go** there next month.

 Winner's Tip! I'll / you'll / he'll / she'll / it'll / we'll / they'll

Part 3B: Fill in the blanks

1. Will _____ go _____ the bus stop tomorrow?
   Yes, he _____. He'll _____ there _____.

2. _____ she _____ to _____ next week?
   No, she _____. _____ won't go there _____.

3. _____ _____ go to _____ next month?
   No, we _____. We won't go _____ _____.

4. Will _____ _____ to _____ later?
   Yes, they _____. _____ go _____ _____.

Part 4A: Verb of the day

go / goes – went – going – gone (йти)

Every afternoon, we __go__ to the train station.

He usually __goes__ to the library with a friend.

Yesterday, we all __went__ to the bus stop.

She is __going__ to the fire station right now.

We have never __gone__ to the factory before.

Part 4B: Verb Practice

1. Every morning, we _____ to the school very early.

2. On Mondays, she _____ to the swimming pool.

3. Every summer, he _____ to the zoo with friends.

4. Last week, I _____ to the fruit market for pears.

5. Yesterday, we _____ to the new department store.

6. Last year, she _____ to Australia for a trip.

7. Right now, I am _____ to the toy store for a doll.

8. We are _____ to the train station right now.

9. She has never _____ South Africa before.

10. We have _____ to many places in this big city.

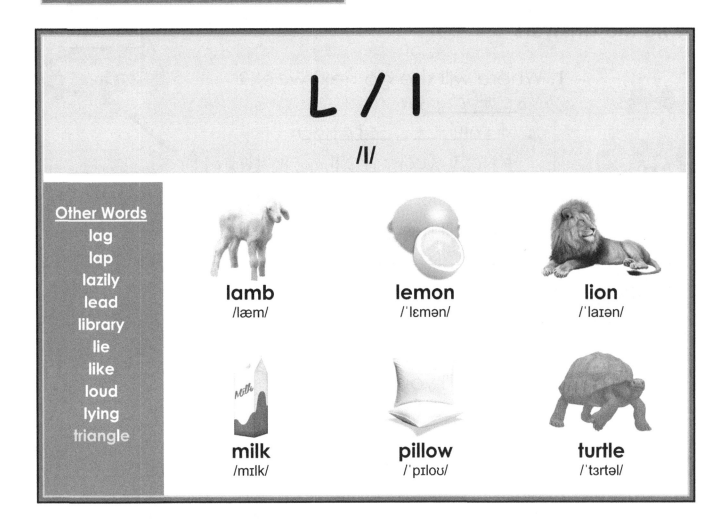

L / l

/l/

Other Words
lag
lap
lazily
lead
library
lie
like
loud
lying
triangle

lamb
/læm/

lemon
/ˈlɛmən/

lion
/ˈlaɪən/

milk
/mɪlk/

pillow
/ˈpɪloʊ/

turtle
/ˈtɜrtəl/

Part 5B: Write and read

1. __oud __ions __ead __agging __ambs.

2. Triang__e __ibrary pi__ows __ie __azi__y.

3. __ying turt__es __ike __apping __emon mi__k.

Write the answers

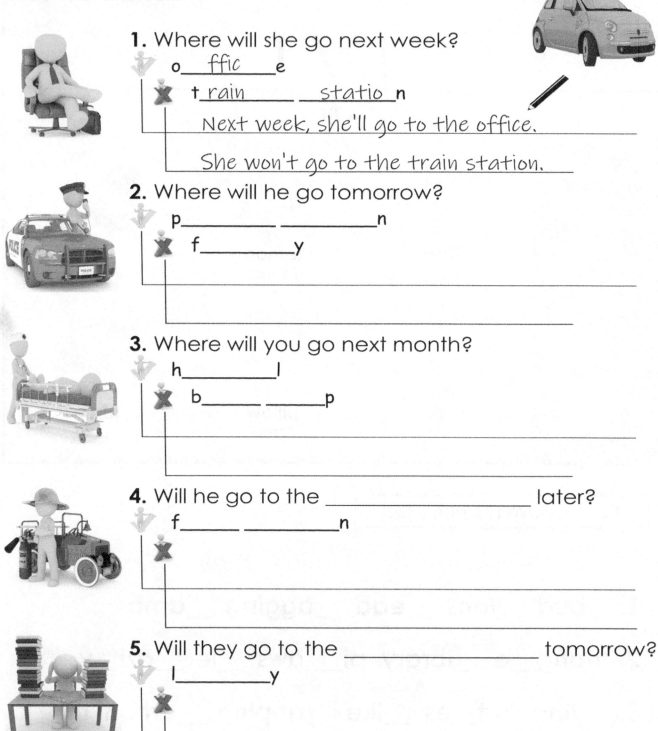

1. Where will she go next week?
   - o___ffic___e
   - t_rain_____ ___statio_n
   - _Next week, she'll go to the office._
   - _She won't go to the train station._

2. Where will he go tomorrow?
   - p_____ _____n
   - f_____y
   - _____
   - _____

3. Where will you go next month?
   - h_____l
   - b_____ _____p
   - _____
   - _____

4. Will he go to the _____ later?
   - f_____ _____n
   - _____
   - _____

5. Will they go to the _____ tomorrow?
   - l_____y
   - _____
   - _____

Lesson 20 — The weather

погода

Part 1A: Learn the words

1. **snowy**
   сніжна
2. **sunny**
   сонячна
3. **rainy**
   дощова
4. **windy**
   вітряна
5. **cloudy**
   марна

6. **hot**
   жарка
7. **cold**
   холодна
8. **warm**
   тепла
9. **cool**
   прохолодна
10. **freezing**
    крижана, морозна

 Practice speaking: "сонячна" is "<u>sunny</u>" in English!

Part 1B: Write the words

Write the missing letters!   Write x 1   Write x 2

1. c__o__d__   _____   _____
2. __o__d   _____   _____
3. c__o__   _____   _____
4. __r__e__i__g   _____   _____
5. __o__   _____   _____
6. r__i__y   _____   _____
7. __n__w__   _____   _____
8. s__n__y   _____   _____
9. __a__m   _____   _____
10. w__n__y   _____   _____

Part 2A: Ask a question

What will the weather be like <u>on Monday</u>?

✓ On Monday, **the weather will be <u>cold</u>. It won't be <u>hot</u>.**

What will the weather be like <u>next week</u>?

✓ Next week, **it will be <u>rainy</u>. It won't be <u>windy</u>.**

 Winner's Tip! on...Monday, Tuesday, Wednesday, Thursday, Friday, Saturday, Sunday

Part 2B: Fill in the blanks

1. What _____ the weather be like _____?
   On Tuesday, _____ will be cool. It won't be _____.

2. _____ will the weather be _____ _____?
   Tomorrow, _____ will be _____. It won't be sunny.

3. What _____ the _____ be like _____?
   Next week, it _____ be windy. It won't be _____.

4. _____ _____ the _____ be like _____?
   On Friday, it will be _____. It _____ be _____.

Will the weather be <u>hot</u> <u>on Thursday</u>?

✓ **Yes, it will be. The weather will be** hot on Thursday.

✗ **No, it won't be. It won't be** hot **that day.**

Will the weather be <u>windy</u> <u>tomorrow</u>?

✓ **Yes, it will be. The weather will be** windy tomorrow.

✗ **No, it won't be. It won't be** windy tomorrow.

Winner's Tip! Answer with "it" for "the weather"

1. _____ the _____ be snowy _____?

   Yes, _____ will be. It _____ be snowy on Monday.

2. Will _____ _____ be rainy tomorrow?

   No, it _____ be. It won't be _____ that day.

3. _____ the _____ be warm _____?

   No, it _____ be. It won't be _____ next week.

4. _____ the _____ be _____ on Thursday?

   _____, it will be. It _____ be sunny that day.

feel / feels – felt – feeling – felt (відчувати)

Often, I <u>feel</u> cold when I sleep at night.

Every summer, it <u>feels</u> very hot outside.

Yesterday, we <u>felt</u> tired after our classes.

She is <u>feeling</u> a little sick after she fell.

I have never <u>felt</u> so happy before!

Part 4B: Verb Practice

1. Every time I take a trip, I _____ very excited.

2. Each time he's sick, he _____ really uncomfortable.

3. On Fridays, she _____ quite tired after work.

4. Last Tuesday, we _____ hot in the sunny weather.

5. Yesterday, I _____ the wind blowing in my hair.

6. This morning, he _____ awake after he had coffee.

7. She is _____ sad now because the weekend is done.

8. We are _____ hot after exercising at the gym.

9. He has never _____ freezing weather before.

10. I have _____ really cold since this morning.

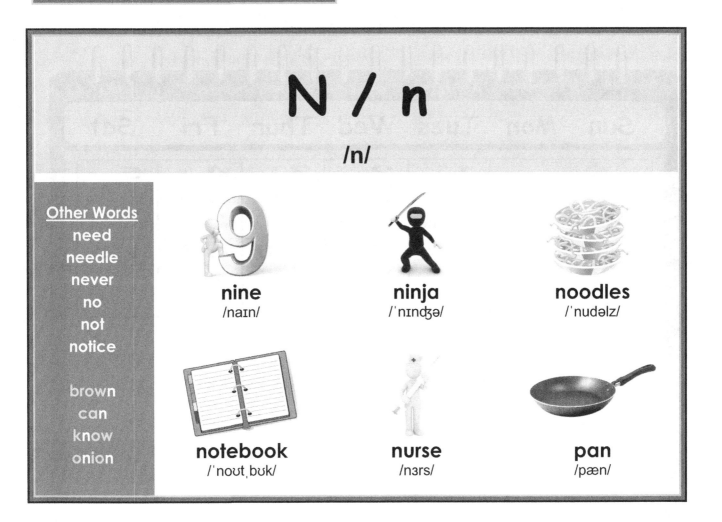

N / n

/n/

Other Words
need
needle
never
no
not
notice

brown
can
know
onion

nine
/naɪn/

ninja
/ˈnɪndʒə/

noodles
/ˈnudəlz/

notebook
/ˈnoʊtˌbʊk/

nurse
/nɜrs/

pan
/pæn/

Part 5B: Write and read

1. __i__e __i__jas __eed __o __otebooks.

2. __urses k__ow __eedles __ot __oodles.

3. __otice pa__ o__io__ ca__ __ever brow__.

Part 6: Fun review

Check the weather and write the answers

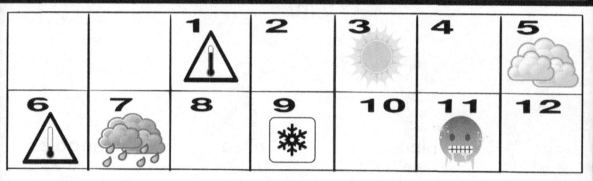

Sun	Mon	Tues	Wed	Thur	Fri	Sat
		1	2	3	4	5
6	7	8	9	10	11	12

1. What will the weather be like on Tuesday?

   <u>On Tuesday, the weather will be hot. It won't be windy.</u>

2. What will the weather be like on Thursday?

   _____

3. What will the weather be like on Saturday?

   _____

4. What will the weather be like on Monday?

   _____

5. Will the weather be cold on Sunday?

   _____

6. Will the weather be warm on Wednesday?

   _____

7. Will the weather be freezing on Friday?

   _____

Write the correct answer next to the letter "A"

A: ___ **1.** Where did you buy _____ pants? I bought _____ online.
a) those / them **b)** these / they
c) these / it **d)** them / those

A: ___ **2.** Where will he _____ later? Later, _____ go to the fire station.
a) goes / he will **b)** go / he's
c) go / he'll **d)** going / he

A: ___ **3.** Will the weather _____ snowy on Friday? No, it _____ be.
a) is / isn't **b)** are / will
c) being / will not **d)** be / won't

A: ___ **4.** What kind of meat _____ he _____ for lunch? He ate ham for lunch.
a) do / eat **b)** is / ate
c) did / eat **d)** did / ate

A: ___ **5.** She always _____ some _____ in the nurse's office.
a) put / marker **b)** puts / markers
c) puts / marker **d)** putting / markers

A: ___ **6.** What _____ the weather _____ like next week?
a) will / be **b)** is / being
c) will / being **d)** is / be

A: ___ **7.** Did you eat salami for _____? Yes, I _____. I ate salami for a snack.
a) snack / did **b)** a snack / did
c) lunch / ate **d)** a snack / ate

A: ___ **8.** Did he _____ a coach in the gym yesterday? Yes, he _____.
a) saw / saw **b)** see / saw
c) sees / does **d)** see / did

A: ___ **9.** Did we buy _____ jeans in Australia? No, we _____.
a) these / don't **b)** these / didn't
c) those / haven't **d)** those / didn't buy

A: ___ **10.** Will you go to the office next week? Yes, I ____. ____ go there then.
a) go / I won't
b) going / I
c) will / I'll
d) will / I

A: ___ **11.** Last weekend, he _____ me _____ boots.
a) lends / those
b) lending / some
c) lent / these
d) lend / any

A: ___ **12.** Where did they _____ the principal last month?
   Last month, they _____ the principal in the computer lab.
a) see / seeing
b) saw / saw
c) see / saw
d) saw / seeing

A: ___ **13.** Last night, _____ _____ dinner late at night with his family.
a) we / eating
b) he / eats
c) you / eat
d) they / ate

A: ___ **14.** _____ usually _____ to the train station with her friends.
a) He / go
b) She / goes
c) They / going
d) She / going

A: ___ **15.** He _____ _____ really cold in this winter weather.
a) is / feels
b) is / feeling
c) has / feel
d) has / feeling

A: ___ **16.** Did she _____ shrimp for dinner? No, she _____.
a) eat / didn't
b) eat / didn't eat
c) have / doesn't
d) ate / don't

A: ___ **17.** Yesterday, we ____ the teacher ____ the pencil in the classroom.
a) saw / put
b) seeing / puts
c) see / putting
d) seen / put

A: ___ **18.** Will the _____ be _____ next week?
a) windy / weather
b) cloudy / warm
c) weather / freezing
d) weather / freeze

Answers on page 257

Lesson 21 School subjects

шкільні предмети

Part 1A: Learn the words

1. **art**
образотворче мистецтво

2. **computer**
інформатика

3. **English**
англійська

4. **geography**
географія

5. **history**
історія

6. **math**
математика

7. **music**
музика

8. **physical education (P.E.)**
фізична культура

9. **science**
природничі науки

10. **social studies**
соціологія

 Practice speaking: "природничі науки " is "_science_" in English!

Part 1B: Write the words

Write the missing letters!   Write x 1   Write x 2

1. __r__ _____ _____
2. c__m__u__e__ _____ _____
3. __n__l__s__ _____ _____
4. g__o__r__p__y _____ _____
5. __i__t__r__ _____ _____
6. m__t__ _____ _____
7. __u__i__ _____ _____
8. __h__sical ed__c__tion _____ _____
9. s__i__n__e _____ _____
10. __o__i__l s__u__i__s _____ _____

When will you have <u>geography</u> class?

✓ **I'll have** geography **class after** <u>math</u> **class.**

✗ **I won't have it before** <u>social studies</u> **class.**

When will she have <u>computer</u> class?

✓ **She'll have it before** <u>physical education</u> **class.**

✗ **She won't have** computer **class after** <u>English</u> **class.**

 **Winner's Tip!** after, before

1. When _____ he _____ history class?

   _____ have _____ class after computer _____.

2. _____ will _____ have P.E. _____?

   They'll _____ it _____ social studies class.

3. _____ will _____ _____ science class?

   I won't _____ science _____ before _____ class.

4. _____ _____ we _____ music _____?

   We _____ have _____ class after _____ class.

Will we have <u>history</u> class after <u>music</u> class?

✓ **Yes, we will. We'll have** history **class after** music **class.**

✗ **No, we won't. We won't have** it **after** music **class.**

Will they have <u>art</u> class before <u>science</u> class?

✓ **Yes, they will. They'll have** art **before** science **class.**

✗ **No, they won't. They won't have** it **before** science **class.**

 Winner's Tip! Answer with "it" for "<u>X</u> Class"

1. Will _____ have P.E. _____ _____ art class?
   Yes, I will. _____ have it before _____ class.

2. _____ she have _____ class after math class?
   Yes, she will. _____ have it _____ _____ class.

3. Will we have _____ class after _____ class?
   No, we won't. We _____ have it after _____ class.

4. Will he have _____ class _____ _____ class?
   Yes, he will. _____ have it before _____ class.

Part 4A: Verb of the day

do / does – did – doing – done (робити)

Every day, I always <u>do</u> my homework.

Sometimes, he <u>does</u> work at the office.

Yesterday, she <u>did</u> art at the beach.

They are <u>doing</u> some math right now.

We have never <u>done</u> our work slowly.

Part 4B: Verb Practice

1. Every evening, I _____ homework before sleeping.
2. On Wednesdays, she _____ work on her computer.
3. Every Sunday, he _____ the dishes in the kitchen.
4. Last class, they _____ a lot of English writing.
5. Last weekend, I _____ lots of work in my new room.
6. This morning, we _____ exercise at the beach.
7. Right now, he is _____ many science projects.
8. We are _____ a social studies test right now.
9. She has never _____ a computer test before.
10. You have _____ a lot of studying this month.

V / v

/v/

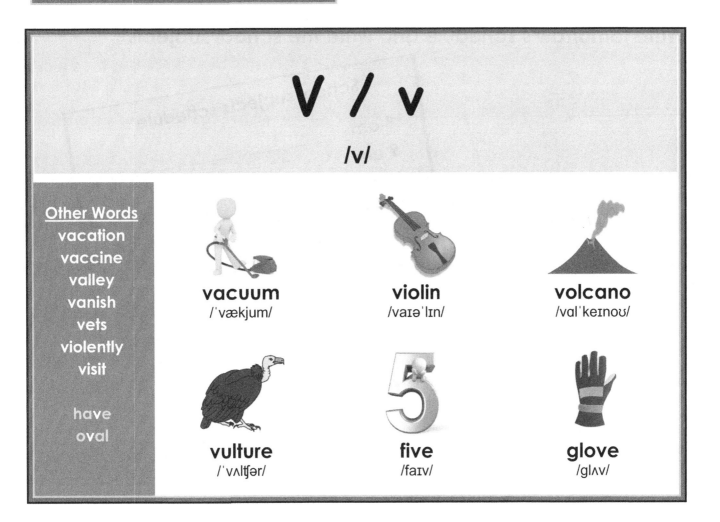

Other Words
vacation
vaccine
valley
vanish
vets
violently
visit

have
oval

vacuum
/'vækjum/

violin
/vaɪə'lɪn/

volcano
/val'keɪnoʊ/

vulture
/'vʌltʃər/

five
/faɪv/

glove
/glʌv/

1. __iolin __ultures __anish __ery __iolently.

2. __accine __ets ha__e __acuumed __olcanoes.

3. Fi__e glo__es __isit o__al __acation __alleys.

Part 6: Fun review

Write tomorrow's schedule and write the school subjects

School subjects schedule

8 am _____
9 am _____
10 am _____
11 am _____ *geography class*
1 pm _____
2 pm _____

English

He'll have a math class after geography class.
We'll have a science class before geography class.
He'll have an English class after math class.
We'll have a music class before P.E. class.
He'll have a P.E. class before science class.

True or False? Circle the answer

1. He'll have a math class before English class.   **True   False**

2. He won't have a history class after music class.   **True   False**

3. He'll have a computer class after science class.   **True   False**

4. We'll have a history class before science class.   **True   False**

Lesson 22 — Sports

спорт

Part 1A: Learn the words

1. **basketball**
   баскетбол
2. **soccer**
   футбол
3. **badminton**
   бадмінтон
4. **golf**
   гольф
5. **hockey**
   хокей

6. **cricket**
   крикет
7. **tennis**
   теніс
8. **baseball**
   бейсбол
9. **volleyball**
   волейбол
10. **football**
    футбол

 Practice speaking: "волейбол" means "<u>volleyball</u>"!

Part 1B: Write the words

Write the missing letters!   Write x 1   Write x 2

1. b _ d _ i _ t _ n   _____   _____
2. _ a _ e _ a _ l   _____   _____
3. b _ s _ e _ b _ l _   _____   _____
4. _ r _ c _ e _   _____   _____
5. f _ o _ b _ l _   _____   _____
6. _ o _ f   _____   _____
7. h _ c _ e _   _____   _____
8. _ o _ c _ r   _____   _____
9. t _ n _ i _   _____   _____
10. _ o _ l _ y _ a _ l   _____   _____

What are you going to play <u>tonight</u>?

✓ Tonight, I'm going to play <u>badminton</u>.

✗ Tonight, I'm not going to play <u>baseball</u>.

What is he going to play <u>next Monday</u>?

✓ Next Monday, he's going to play <u>cricket</u>.

✗ Next Monday, he's not going to play <u>tennis</u>.

 Winner's Tip! Use: later, tomorrow, next week, etc.

Part 2B: Fill in the blanks

1. What _____ you _____ to _____ next week?
   Next week, _____ going _____ play hockey.

2. _____ is _____ going to play _____?
   Later, she's not _____ to _____ badminton.

3. What _____ they _____ to play _____?
   Next Tuesday, _____ going to _____ football.

4. _____ are _____ _____ to play _____?
   Tomorrow, we're not _____ to _____ _____.

Part 3A: Yes / No questions

Are you going to play <u>basketball</u> <u>tomorrow</u>?

✓ **Yes, I am. I'm going to play** basketball tomorrow.
✗ **No, I'm not. I'm not going to play** basketball tomorrow.

Is she going to play <u>golf</u> <u>next week</u>?

✓ **Yes, she is. She's going to play** golf next week.
✗ **No, she's not. She isn't going to play** golf next week.

 Winner's Tip! I'm, you're, he's, she's, it's, we're, they're

Part 3B: Fill in the blanks

1. Are _____ _____ to play _____ next week?
   Yes, we are. _____ going to play volleyball _____.

2. Is _____ going to play _____ _____?
   Yes, he is. _____ going to _____ tennis tomorrow.

3. _____ you going to _____ baseball _____?
   No, _____ not. I'm not going to play _____ later.

4. Is _____ _____ to play _____ tonight?
   No, she's not. She _____ going to play cricket _____.

137

Part 4A: Verb of the day

play / plays – played – playing – played (грати)

Every day, I always <u>play</u> with my toys.

He usually <u>plays</u> basketball with friends.

Yesterday, she <u>played</u> music loudly.

We are <u>playing</u> a fun game right now.

We have never <u>played</u> golf very well.

Part 4B: Verb Practice

1. Every morning, I _____ music on my computer.
2. On Mondays, she _____ hockey at the park.
3. Every week, he _____ many sports at the school.
4. Last time, you _____ baseball for a long time.
5. Last Tuesday, I _____ many different video games.
6. This morning, we _____ volleyball at the beach.
7. Right now, she is _____ on a basketball team.
8. They're _____ the game very well right now.
9. They have never _____ cricket before.
10. She has _____ a lot of tennis this month.

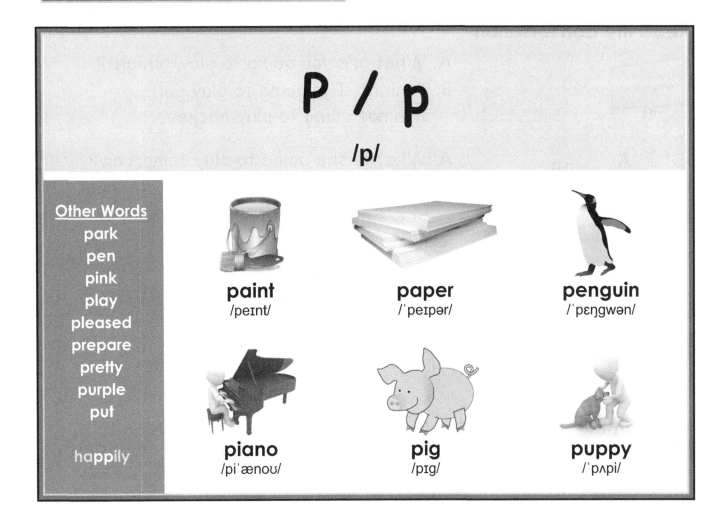

P / p

/p/

Other Words
park
pen
pink
play
pleased
prepare
pretty
purple
put

happily

paint
/peɪnt/

paper
/ˈpeɪpər/

penguin
/ˈpɛŋgwən/

piano
/piˈænoʊ/

pig
/pɪg/

puppy
/ˈpʌpi/

1. __ink __igs ha___ily __ut in __ark __ens.

2. __aper __u__ies __re__are __ur__le __aint.

3. __leased __enguins __lay __retty __iano.

Read the conversation

A: What are you going to play tonight?
B: Tonight, I'm going to play golf.
I'm not going to play hockey.

A: What is she going to play tomorrow?
B: Tomorrow, she's going to play tennis.
She's not going to play volleyball.

A: Are you going to play football next week?
B: Yes, I am. I'm going to play football next week.

A: Is he going to play basketball later?
B: No, he's not. He isn't going to play basketball later.

Unscramble the words. Circle only the sports they are going to play

OFLG	OIMBANTND	STENIN
golf		
LAEATSKLBB	OYCEKH	ABBSELLA
ECCROS	TECCIRK	LBVLELLYAO
	OOLLABTF	

Lesson 23 At the ice cream shop

в кафе-морозиві

Part 1A: Learn the words

1. **chocolate**
   шоколад
2. **strawberry**
   полуниця
3. **mint**
   м'ята
4. **raspberry**
   малина
5. **cherry**
   вишня

6. **vanilla**
   ваніль
7. **coffee**
   кава
8. **almond**
   мигдаль
9. **caramel**
   карамель
10. **coconut**
    кокос

 Practice speaking: "м'ята " is "<u>mint</u>" in English!

Part 1B: Write the words

Write the missing letters!   Write x 1   Write x 2

1. _h_c_l_t_ _____ _____
2. v_n_l_a _____ _____
3. _t_a_b_r_y _____ _____
4. a_m_n_ _____ _____
5. _a_a_e_ _____ _____
6. c_e_r_ _____ _____
7. _o_o_u_ _____ _____
8. c_f_e_ _____ _____
9. _i_t _____ _____
10. r_s_b_r_y _____ _____

Which flavor are you going to have?

✓ I'm going to have <u>raspberry</u> flavor.
✗ I'm not going to have <u>vanilla</u> flavor.

Which flavor is she going to have?

✓ She's going to have <u>coconut</u> flavor.
✗ She's not going to have <u>almond</u> flavor.

 Winner's Tip! "Which": used for limited options

Part 2B: Fill in the blanks

1. which _____ are _____ going to _____?
   We _____ _____ to have vanilla flavor.

2. _____ flavor _____ they _____ to have?
   _____ aren't going to _____ cherry _____.

3. _____ flavor _____ he going to _____?
   He's _____ to _____ caramel _____.

4. which _____ are _____ _____ to have?
   I'm not _____ to _____ _____ flavor.

Are you going to have <u>chocolate</u> flavor?

✓ **Yes, I am. I'm going to have** chocolate **flavor.**

✗ **No, I'm not. I'm not going to have** chocolate **flavor.**

Is she going to have <u>strawberry</u> flavor?

✓ **Yes, she is. She's going to have** strawberry **flavor.**

✗ **No, she's not. She isn't going to have** strawberry **flavor.**

 Winner's Tip! Remember: "are" or "is"

Part 3B: Fill in the blanks

1. Is he _____ to _____ the caramel _____?
Yes, he is. _____ going to have the _____ flavor.

2. Is _____ _____ to have the _____ flavor?
Yes, she is. She's _____ to have the mint _____.

3. Are _____ going to have the _____ _____?
No, we _____. We're not going to have the almond flavor.

4. Are _____ going to have the _____ _____?
Yes, I am. I'm _____ to _____ the cherry flavor.

have / has – had – having – had (мати)

Every morning, I always <u>have</u> hot coffee.

He usually <u>has</u> vegetables for dinner.

Yesterday, she <u>had</u> some mint ice cream.

He is <u>having</u> problems understanding.

They have never <u>had</u> a lot of money.

Part 4B: Verb Practice

1. Every day, I _____ football practice at the park.

2. On Saturdays, she always _____ many things to do.

3. Every month, he _____ lots of computer homework.

4. Last time, we _____ some ice cream at the beach.

5. Last Thursday, I _____ a few problems at school.

6. Yesterday, they _____ different flavors of coffee.

7. Right now, she is _____ a fun time at the market.

8. They're _____ a really big pizza party right now.

9. They have never _____ a lot of luck before.

10. He has _____ many different jobs before this one.

ng

/ŋ/

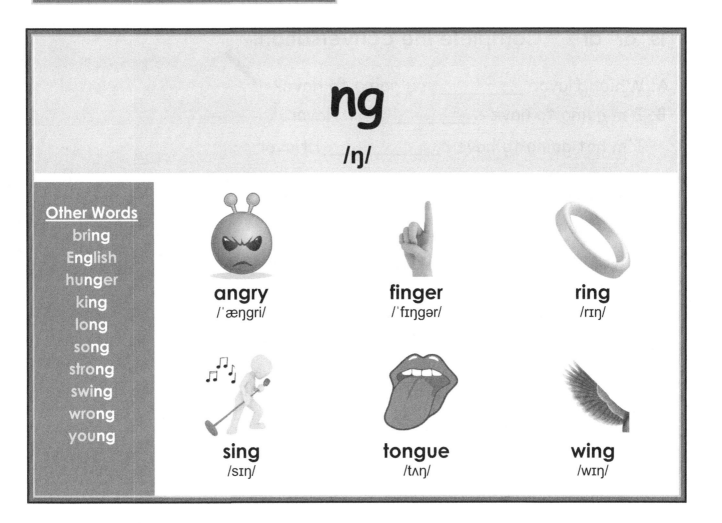

Other Words
bring
English
hunger
king
long
song
strong
swing
wrong
young

angry
/ˈæŋgri/

finger
/ˈfɪŋgər/

ring
/rɪŋ/

sing
/sɪŋ/

tongue
/tʌŋ/

wing
/wɪŋ/

Part 5B: Write and read

1. A___ry ki___s si___ lo___ so___s.

2. Stro___ fi___er ri___s swi___ you___ wi___s.

3. Wro___ E___lish to___ues bri___ hu___er.

"Is" or "are"? Complete the conversation.

A: Which flavor _____ you going to have?

B: I'm going to have c_____t flavor.

I'm not going to have c_____l flavor.

A: Which flavor _____ she going to have?

B: She's going to have a_____d flavor.

She's not going to have c_____y flavor.

A: Which flavor _____ they going to have?

B: They're going to have v_____a flavor.

He's not going to have r_____y flavor.

A: Which flavor _____ he going to have?

B: He's going to have s_____y flavor.

m
i
n
t

Lesson 24 Activities

діяльність

Part 1A: Learn the words

1. **play piano**
   грати на піаніно
2. **read books**
   читати книги
3. **play video games**
   грати у відео ігри
4. **surf the internet**
   шукати в Інтернеті
5. **take photos**
   Фотографувати

6. **watch TV**
   дивитись телевізор
7. **sing songs**
   співати пісні
8. **study English**
   вивчати англійську
9. **play cards**
   грати в карти
10. **go shopping**
    ходити за покупками

 Practice speaking: "читати книги " means "<u>read books</u>"!

Part 1B: Write the words

Write the missing letters!   Write x 1   Write x 2

1. g__ _h_p_i_g   _____   _____
2. _l_y _a_d_   _____   _____
3. p_a_ p_a_o   _____   _____
4. play v_d_o g_m_s   _____   _____
5. _e_d b_o_s   _____   _____
6. s_n_ s_n_s   _____   _____
7. _t_d_ E_g_i_h   _____   _____
8. s_r_ t_e i_t_rn_t   _____   _____
9. __a_e _h_t_s   _____   _____
10. w_t_h _V   _____   _____

147

What are you going to do <u>this weekend</u>?

✓ This weekend, I'm going to <u>play cards</u>.
✗ This weekend, I'm not going to <u>watch TV</u>.

What is she going to do <u>later</u>?

✓ Later, she's going to <u>study English</u>.
✗ Later, she isn't going to <u>surf the internet</u>.

 Winner's Tip! Use: this weekend, tomorrow, later, tonight

Part 2B: Fill in the blanks

1. _____ are _____ going to do _____?
   Tomorrow, I'm _____ to take photos.

2. What _____ _____ going to do this weekend?
   _____, he's _____ _____ play video games.

3. _____ are _____ going to do _____?
   Later, _____ not _____ _____ play cards.

4. _____ is _____ _____ to do _____?
   Tonight, she isn't _____ to _____.

Part 3A: Yes / No questions

Are we going to <u>sing songs</u> <u>tomorrow</u>?

✓ Yes, we are. We're going to sing songs tomorrow.

✗ No, we're not. We aren't going to sing songs tomorrow.

Is he going to <u>go shopping</u> <u>tonight</u>?

✓ Yes, he is. He's going to go shopping tonight.

✗ No, he isn't. He isn't going to go shopping tonight.

 Winner's Tip! Remember: they're = they are, etc.

Part 3B: Fill in the blanks

1. _____ you going to play video games _____?
   Yes, I _____. I'm _____ to play video games later.

2. _____ she _____ to read books _____?
   No, _____ isn't. She _____ going to read books tonight.

3. Is _____ _____ to take photos _____?
   No, he isn't. _____ isn't _____ to take photos later.

4. Are _____ _____ _____ play piano tomorrow?
   Yes, they are. _____ _____ to play piano _____.

read / reads – read – reading – read (читати)

Every morning, I <u>read</u> my favorite books.

He usually <u>reads</u> stories to his younger sister.

Last year, he <u>read</u> a book about cooking.

We are <u>reading</u> about grammar right now.

They have never <u>read</u> any scary books.

Part 4B: Verb Practice

1. Every weekend, I _____ a new book at the park.
2. Each Friday, he _____ about exercise and health.
3. Every week, he _____ about different countries.
4. Last time, we _____ stories about zoo animals.
5. Yesterday, I _____ an email from my best friend.
6. Last night, we _____ something about ice cream.
7. Right now, she is _____ her favorite kind of book.
8. They are _____ many different subjects at school.
9. She has never _____ a newspaper before.
10. He has _____ a lot of travel information already.

ar

/ar/

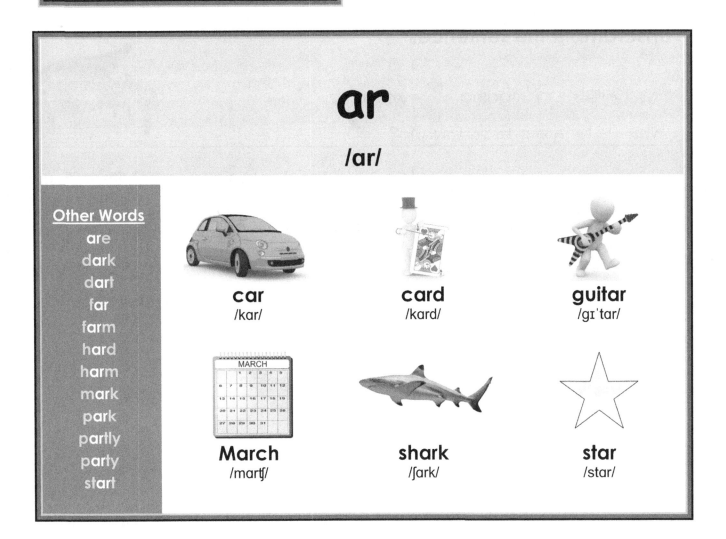

Other Words
are
dark
dart
far
farm
hard
harm
mark
park
partly
party
start

car
/kar/

card
/kard/

guitar
/gɪˈtar/

March
/martʃ/

shark
/ʃark/

star
/star/

1. F___m c___s ___e p___ked p___tly f___.

2. D___k d___ts h___m guit___ c___d sh___ks.

3. M___ch st___s m___k h___d p___ty st___ts.

Part 6: Fun review

Unscramble the sentences

tonight do going is what to he

1. __what is he going to do tonight?__

piano going play he's tonight to

_____

this do we what are going to weekend

2. _____

aren't weekend internet going this we to the surf

_____

to they go going are tomorrow shopping

3. _____

to shopping not go tomorrow no aren't they going they're

_____

she cards later going to is play

4. _____

she later cards going is play to yes she's

_____

Lesson 25
In the bathroom

у ванні

1. **mirror**
   дзеркало
2. **bath towel**
   рушник
3. **shower**
   душ
4. **toilet paper**
   туалетний папір
5. **bath mat**
   килимок для ванної

6. **shelf**
   полиця
7. **sink**
   раковина
8. **toilet**
   туалет
9. **bathtub**
   ванна
10. **soap**
   мило

 Practice speaking: "полиця " is "<u>shelf</u>" in English!

Part 1B: Write the words

Write the missing letters!   Write x 1   Write x 2

1. b_t_ m_t   _____   _____
2. _a_h _o_e_   _____   _____
3. b_t_t_b   _____   _____
4. _i_r_r   _____   _____
5. s_e_f   _____   _____
6. _h_w_r   _____   _____
7. s_n_   _____   _____
8. _o_p   _____   _____
9. t_i_e_   _____   _____
10. _o_l_t p_p_r _____   _____

When are you going to <u>clean</u> the <u>toilet</u>?

✓ I'm going to clean the toilet <u>at seven o'clock</u>.

✗ I'm not going to clean the toilet <u>at eight o'clock</u>.

When is he going to <u>buy</u> the <u>toilet paper</u>?

✓ He's going to buy the toilet paper <u>at eleven o'clock</u>.

✗ He's not going to buy the it <u>at twelve o'clock</u>.

 Winner's Tip! Learn: o'clock / Use: numbers 1-12

1. _____ are you _____ to _____ the bath mat?
_____ not going to buy the _____ at one o'clock.

2. _____ is _____ going to clean the _____?
She's _____ to _____ the bathtub at three o'clock.

3. when _____ we _____ to _____ the shelf?
_____ not _____ to buy the _____ at six o'clock.

4. _____ is _____ going to _____ the sink?
He's _____ to clean the _____ _____.

Are we going to <u>wash</u> the <u>shower</u> <u>at two o'clock</u>?

✓ **Yes, we are. We're going to** wash it at two o'clock.

✗ **No, we're not. We're not going to** wash it at two o'clock.

Is she going to <u>clean</u> the <u>sink</u> <u>at ten o'clock</u>?

✓ **Yes, she is. She's going to** clean it at ten o'clock.

✗ **No, she's not. She isn't going to** clean it at ten o'clock.

 Winner's Tip! Use verbs: clean, wash, buy

Part 3B: Fill in the blanks

1. Are you _____ to wash the bath towel _____?
Yes, I am. _____ going to _____ it at one o'clock.

2. Is _____ going to _____ the soap at four o'clock?
No, he's _____. He isn't going to buy it _____.

3. Is she _____ to clean the mirror _____?
No, _____ not. She isn't going to _____ it at two o'clock.

4. Are we going to _____ the _____ _____?
Yes, we are. We're _____ to clean the shower at five o'clock.

wash / washes – washed – washing – washed (мити)

Every day, I <u>wash</u> my hair in the shower.

He often <u>washes</u> his car on sunny days.

Last week, we <u>washed</u> the bathtub well.

We are <u>washing</u> some clothes right now.

They have never <u>washed</u> any vegetables.

Part 4B: Verb Practice

1. Every Saturday, I _____ all of my dirty clothes.
2. On Wednesdays, she _____ her bicycle very well.
3. Every day, he often _____ his hands with soap.
4. Yesterday, they _____ their friend's new car.
5. Last week, I _____ many dishes in the kitchen.
6. At his old job, he _____ monkeys at the zoo.
7. Right now, he is _____ his jacket that got dirty.
8. They are _____ everything that's in the sink.
9. He has never _____ his hat before, so it's stinky.
10. We have _____ the mirror and sink many times.

sh

/ʃ/

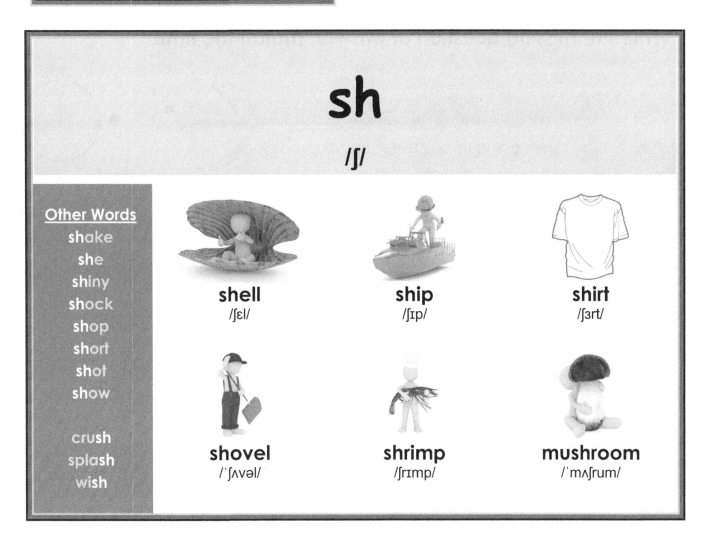

Other Words
shake
she
shiny
shock
shop
short
shot
show

crush
splash
wish

shell
/ʃɛl/

ship
/ʃɪp/

shirt
/ʃɜrt/

shovel
/ˈʃʌvəl/

shrimp
/ʃrɪmp/

mushroom
/ˈmʌʃrum/

Part 5B: Write and read

1. ___e wi___es ___ops ___owed ___ort ___irts.

2. ___aking ___rimp spla___ ___iny ___ot ___ells.

3. Cru___ed ___oveled mu___rooms ___ock ___ips.

Write the missing question or answer, match the time

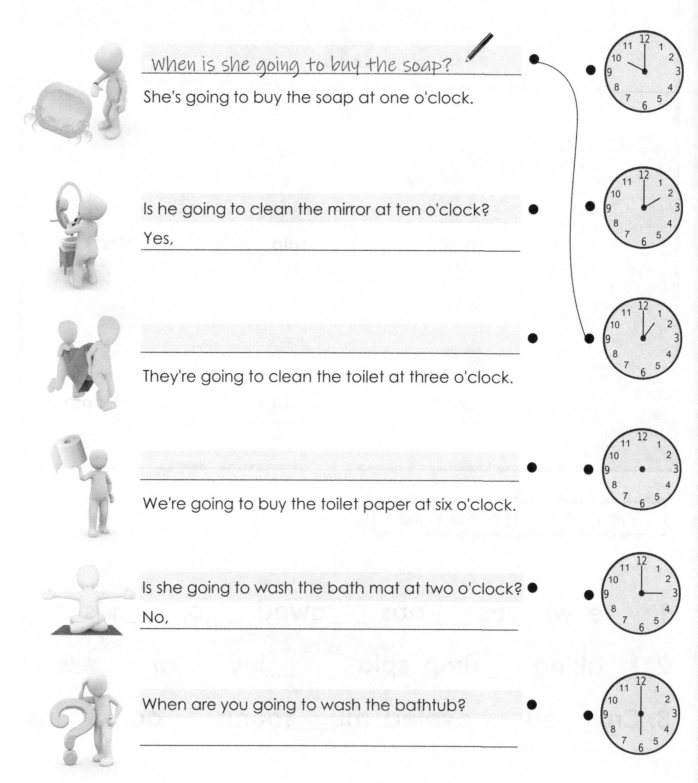

When is she going to buy the soap?

She's going to buy the soap at one o'clock.

Is he going to clean the mirror at ten o'clock?

Yes,

They're going to clean the toilet at three o'clock.

We're going to buy the toilet paper at six o'clock.

Is she going to wash the bath mat at two o'clock?

No,

When are you going to wash the bathtub?

Write the correct answer next to the letter "A"

A: ___ **1.** _____ going to buy the soap at eight _____.
a) He'll / tonight
b) He / thirty
c) He's / clock
d) He's / o'clock

A: ___ **2.** _____ weekend, _____ not going to play video games.
a) Over / he'll
b) On / she's
c) This / she's
d) The / he

A: ___ **3.** _____ not going to _____ raspberry flavor.
a) He's / has
b) We've / have
c) She'll / have
d) She's / have

A: ___ **4.** Next Tuesday, _____ not going to _____ hockey.
a) he's / play
b) he / play
c) he will / playing
d) he'll / plays

A: ___ **5.** _____ have computer class _____ geography class.
a) She / after
b) She'll / before
c) She's / before
d) She will / between

A: ___ **6.** Every morning, _____ usually _____ black coffee for breakfast.
a) I / has
b) I / have
c) he / having
d) you / are have

A: ___ **7.** No, _____ not. We _____ going to _____ songs tomorrow.
a) it's / are not / singing
b) we are / 're not / sang
c) we're / aren't / sing
d) we / are not / singing

A: ___ **8.** _____ he going to _____ the shower at three o'clock?
a) Will / clean
b) Won't / cleans
c) Isn't / cleaning
d) is / clean

A: ___ **9.** No, we _____. We won't _____ art class after music class.
a) don't / having
b) can't / had
c) won't / have
d) won't / has

A: ___ 10. _____ you going to _____ badminton tomorrow?
a) Are / play   **b)** Do / playing
c) Will / play   **d)** Are / playing

A: ___ 11. She often _____ _____ before sleeping every night.
a) reads / books   **b)** read / books
c) reading / a book   **d)** reads / book

A: ___ 12. Right now, they _____ _____ his car before it gets dark outside.
a) have / washes   **b)** can / washing
c) are / wash   **d)** are / washing

A: ___ 13. She _____ never _____ her history homework on time.
a) have / doing   **b)** has / done
c) is / do   **d)** is / did

A: ___ 14. _____ usually _____ tennis at the park near my house.
a) They / play   **b)** We / playing
c) I / plays   **d)** She / play

A: ___ 15. Are you going to have cherry flavor?
          Yes, I _____. _____ going to have cherry flavor.
a) will / I'll   **b)** am / I'm
c) have / I've   **d)** can / I'll

A: ___ 16. What is he going to _____ later? Later, he's going to _____ photos.
a) doing / taking   **b)** do / take
c) done / taken   **d)** did / took

A: ___ 17. He always _____ the dishes before he _____.
a) washes / sleeps   **b)** wash / sleep
c) washing / sleeping   **d)** washed / sleep

A: ___ 18. _____ they have science class after English class?
          No, they won't. They won't have it _____ English class.
a) Do / before   **b)** Are / after
c) Can / before   **d)** Will / after

Answers on page 257

Lesson 26 In the toolbox

в ящику для інструментів

Part 1A: Learn the words

1. **hammer**
   молоток
2. **electric drill**
   електрична дриль
3. **screwdriver**
   викрутка
4. **paintbrush**
   кисть
5. **shovel**
   лопата

6. **tape measure**
   рулетка
7. **axe**
   сокира
8. **pliers**
   плоскогубці
9. **ladder**
   драбина
10. **wrench**
    гайковий ключ

 Practice speaking: "молоток" means "_hammer_"!

Part 1B: Write the words

Write the missing letters!   Write x 1   Write x 2

1. __x__   _____   _____
2. e__e__t__i__ d__i__l   _____   _____
3. __a__m__r   _____   _____
4. l__d__e__   _____   _____
5. __a__n__b__u__h   _____   _____
6. p__i__r__   _____   _____
7. __c__e__d__i__e__   _____   _____
8. s__o__e__   _____   _____
9. t__p__ m__a__u__e   _____   _____
10. __r__n__h   _____   _____

What were you using to fix the <u>shelf</u>?

✓ **I was using the <u>ladder</u> to fix the** shelf.

✗ **I wasn't using the <u>electric drill</u> to fix the** shelf.

What was she using to fix the <u>sink</u>?

✓ **She was using the <u>wrench</u> to fix the** sink.

✗ **She wasn't using the <u>pliers</u> to fix the** sink.

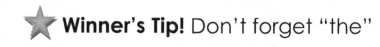 **Winner's Tip!** Don't forget "the"

Part 2B: Fill in the blanks

1. what _____ he _____ to _____ the car?
   _____ was using _____ wrench to fix the _____.

2. _____ was she using _____ fix the _____?
   _____ wasn't _____ the axe to _____ the shower.

3. what _____ they _____ to fix the _____?
   _____ weren't _____ the shovel to fix the bus.

4. _____ _____ we using to _____ the bicycle?
   We _____ using the _____ to fix the _____.

Were you using the <u>screwdriver</u> to fix the <u>mirror</u>?

✓ **Yes, I was. I was using the** screwdriver **to fix the** mirror.
✗ **No, I wasn't. I wasn't using** it **to fix the** mirror.

Was he using the <u>hammer</u> to fix the <u>toilet</u>?

✓ **Yes, he was. He was using the** hammer **to fix the** toilet.
✗ **No, he wasn't. He wasn't using** it **to fix the** toilet.

 Winner's Tip! Answer with "it" instead

Part 3B: Fill in the blanks

1. _____ he using the electric drill to fix the _____?
   Yes, he _____. He was _____ it to fix the taxi.

2. _____ they _____ the ladder to fix the _____?
   No, they _____. They _____ using it to fix the house.

3. Was _____ using the _____ to fix the bathroom?
   No, she _____. She wasn't using it to fix the _____.

4. Were _____ using the _____ to fix the TV?
   Yes, I _____. I was _____ it to _____ the TV.

use / uses – used – using – used (використовувати)

I always <u>use</u> a hammer to fix things.

Every day, she <u>uses</u> her tools at work.

Last week, he <u>used</u> your paintbrush.

They are <u>using</u> the old ladder right now.

You have <u>used</u> this many times before.

Part 4B: Verb Practice

1. Every class, I _____ a pencil and an eraser a lot.

2. In wintertime, she _____ a scarf to keep warm.

3. On hot days, he _____ lemons to make a cold drink.

4. Last time, we _____ a ladder to paint the house.

5. Last weekend, they _____ my car to take a trip.

6. This morning, I _____ some glue to fix my book.

7. Right now, he is _____ some soap to wash the sink.

8. They are _____ English to speak to each other.

9. I have never _____ an axe to cut down a tree.

10. She has _____ the screwdriver many times before.

Z / z + s

/z/

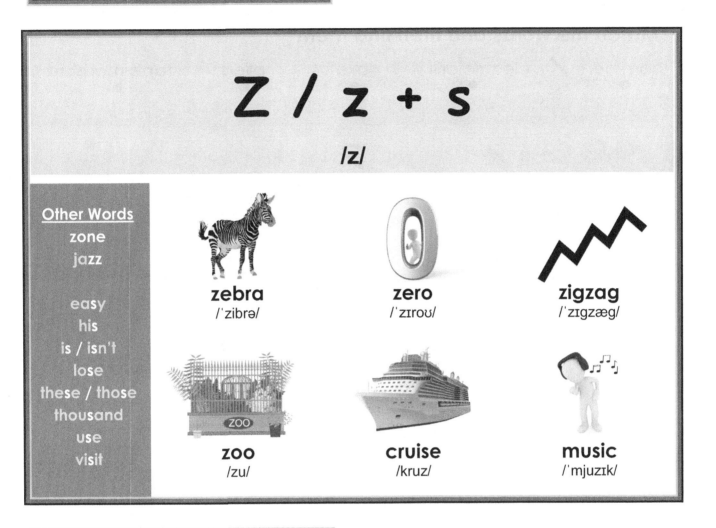

Other Words
zone
jazz

easy
his
is / isn't
lose
these / those
thousand
use
visit

zebra
/ˈzibrə/

zero
/ˈzɪroʊ/

zigzag
/ˈzɪgzæg/

zoo
/zu/

cruise
/kruz/

music
/ˈmjuzɪk/

1. __ero __oo__ lo__e the__e thou__and __ebra__.

2. Vi__iting hi__ ja___ mu__ic i__n't ea__y.

3. Crui__e__ __u__e __ooming __ig__ag __ones.

Match the words and then find them

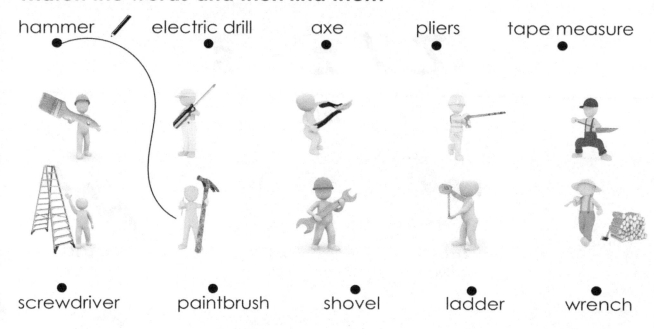

hammer ✏ electric drill   axe   pliers   tape measure

screwdriver   paintbrush   shovel   ladder   wrench

Practice speaking:

"He was using the _hammer_ to fix the _desk_ ."

```
o d h q y o z t e j t i i z k l u g n m x j f y i h a d
d l u p f i l e x g m e t u l b k i p o p e c m q c r z
m c a k d i n t h e t o o l b o x k q x s h l i q c v s
m v y p l i e r s y i k i m h h z g s h o v e l t m q q
w r t j g o l q r n s r r e f w s c r e w d r i v e r z
l v b x m f m e c m d x x w i n n e r s e n g l i s h f
d a f w o p m a c c d a q k a j m p h t c o p f a c x a
y i k d c m q k i h d k l e r w i d m q d j q e s n s c
m s b z a z o r m z t a p e m e a s u r e c l z s n p o
z s r h k x t f b v z o d q a p d f e w n u u d i g a e
e v d f u c w r l j t d q p a i n t b r u s h j a x n x
h i g y e m y b d c a e y i h j f e i j z j n g g a n m
q f i l k g c c x l y w n p h e z n m n v v j h y k e q
a e e g y w r e n c h h a r d h a t w i x p x l v x r z
```

Lesson 27 At the cinema

в кінотеатрі

Part 1A: Learn the words

1. **scary**
   страшний
2. **exciting**
   захоплюючий
3. **informative**
   інформативний
4. **romantic**
   романтичний
5. **violent**
   зі сценами насилля

6. **boring**
   нудний
7. **interesting**
   цікавий
8. **funny**
   смішний
9. **enjoyable**
   приємний
10. **sad**
    сумний

 Practice speaking: "приємний " is "*enjoyable*" in English!

Part 1B: Write the words

Write the missing letters!   Write x 1   Write x 2

1. b__r__n__   _____   _____
2. __n__o__a__l__   _____   _____
3. e__c__t__n__   _____   _____
4. __u__n__   _____   _____
5. i__f__r__a__i__e   _____   _____
6. __n__e__e__t__n__   _____   _____
7. r__m__n__i   _____   _____
8. __a__   _____   _____
9. s__a__y   _____   _____
10. __i__l__n__   _____   _____

How did you feel about the <u>horror</u> movie?

✓ I felt that the horror movie was <u>funny</u>.

✗ I felt that it wasn't <u>scary</u>.

How did he feel about the <u>action</u> movie?

✓ He felt that it was <u>exciting</u>.

✗ He felt that the action movie wasn't <u>boring</u>.

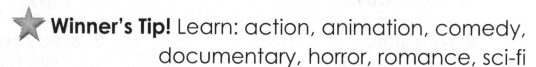 **Winner's Tip!** Learn: action, animation, comedy, documentary, horror, romance, sci-fi

1. How did _____ feel _____ the animation _____?
   They _____ that the _____ movie wasn't enjoyable.

2. _____ did she _____ about the documentary movie?
   _____ felt _____ it _____ informative.

3. How _____ _____ feel about the comedy movie?
   I _____ _____ it wasn't _____.

4. _____ did you _____ about the _____ movie?
   I _____ that the horror movie _____ scary.

Did you feel that the <u>romance</u> movie was <u>romantic</u>?

✓ **Yes, I did. I felt that it was romantic.**

✗ **No, I didn't. I didn't feel that it was romantic.**

Did she feel that the <u>sci-fi</u> movie was <u>interesting</u>?

✓ **Yes, she did. She felt that it was interesting.**

✗ **No, she didn't. She didn't feel that it was interesting.**

 Winner's Tip! Use "it" in your answer

Part 3B: Fill in the blanks

1. Did he feel that the _____ movie was _____?
   Yes, _____ did. He _____ _____ it was violent.

2. _____ she feel that the comedy movie was _____?
   No, she _____. She _____ feel it _____ romantic.

3. Did _____ feel that the action movie was _____?
   _____, I did. I _____ _____ it was funny.

4. _____ they feel _____ the sci-fi _____ was sad?
   Yes, _____ did. _____ felt that it was _____.

teach / teaches – taught – teaching – taught (вчити)

I always <u>teach</u> music to my younger sister.

Every weekend, she <u>teaches</u> us science.

Last year, he <u>taught</u> history at our school.

They are <u>teaching</u> English to us right now.

We have never <u>taught</u> math before.

Part 4B: Verb Practice

1. Every evening, I _____ my nephew how to sing.

2. On Tuesdays, she _____ us how to speak French.

3. Every week, he _____ us some interesting history.

4. Last year at the pool, he _____ me how to swim.

5. Last week, I _____ them about a scary story.

6. This morning, she _____ us how to play piano.

7. Right now, he is _____ them how to take photos.

8. We are _____ from an informative book right now.

9. He has never _____ an exciting class before.

10. I have _____ her about many countries already.

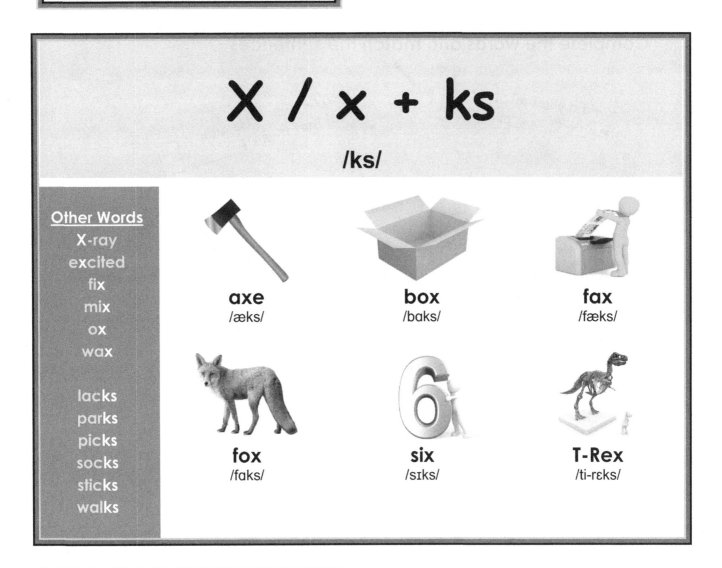

X / x + ks

/ks/

Other Words
X-ray
excited
fix
mix
ox
wax

lacks
parks
picks
socks
sticks
walks

axe
/æks/

box
/baks/

fax
/fæks/

fox
/faks/

six
/sɪks/

T-Rex
/ti-rɛks/

Part 5B: Write and read

1. The fa__ bo__ lac___ __-rayed fo__ soc___.

2. E__cited T-Re__ pic___ wal___ in par___.

3. Si__ mi__ed stic___ fi__ o__'s wa__ a__e.

Part 6: Fun review

Complete the words and match the sentences

How did you feel about the s_ci-fi_____ movie? [1]

No, he didn't. He didn't feel that it was f_____y. [ ]

How did they feel about the h_____ movie? [ ]

How did she feel about the a_____ movie? [ ]

Yes, I did. I felt that it was e_____g. [ ]

Did you feel that the c_____ movie was e_____g? [ ]

Did he feel that the r_____ movie was f_____y? [ ]

I felt that it was i_____g. [1]

They felt that it wasn't s_____y. [ ]

She felt that it was v_____t. [ ]

Lesson 28 At the supermarket

в супермаркеті

Part 1A: Learn the words

1. **milk**
молоко

2. **juice**
сік

3. **meat**
м'ясо

4. **drinks**
напої

5. **vegetables**
овочі

6. **ice cream**
морозиво

7. **fruit**
фрукти

8. **bread**
хліб

9. **fish**
риба

10. **pizza**
піца

 Practice speaking: "овочі" is "_vegetables_" in English!

Part 1B: Write the words

Write the missing letters!   Write x 1   Write x 2

1. __r__a__   _____   _____
2. d__i__k__   _____   _____
3. __i__h   _____   _____
4. f__u__t   _____   _____
5. __c__ c__e__m   _____   _____
6. j__i__e   _____   _____
7. __e__t   _____   _____
8. m__l__   _____   _____
9. __i__z__   _____   _____
10. v__g__t__b__e__   _____   _____

173

What was <u>cheaper</u> than the <u>meat</u>?

✓ **The <u>fish</u> was cheaper than the meat.**

What was <u>more expensive</u> than the <u>juice</u>?

✓ **The <u>milk</u> was more expensive than the juice.**

 Winner's Tip! Learn: cheaper, more expensive

Part 2B: Fill in the blanks

1. _____ was _____ than _____ ice cream?
   The pizza _____ cheaper _____ the _____.

2. What _____ more expensive _____ the _____?
   _____ meat was _____ than _____ bread.

3. What were more _____ than _____ vegetables?
   The drinks were _____ expensive than the _____.

4. _____ was _____ than the _____?
   _____ fruit _____ cheaper _____ the milk.

Was the <u>bread</u> <u>more expensive</u> than the <u>fruit</u>?

✓ **Yes, it was. It was** more expensive **than the** fruit.

X **No, it wasn't. It wasn't** more expensive **than the** fruit.

Were the <u>vegetables</u> <u>cheaper</u> than the <u>drinks</u>?

✓ **Yes, they were. They were** cheaper **than the** drinks.

X **No, they weren't. They weren't** cheaper **than the** drinks.

 Winner's Tip! it (singular), they (plural)

Part 3B: Fill in the blanks

1. Was the meat more expensive _____ the _____?
Yes, it _____. It was _____ than the fruit.

2. _____ the drinks _____ than the vegetables?
Yes, they were. They _____ cheaper than the _____.

3. _____ the bread _____ than the _____?
_____, it was. It _____ cheaper _____ the fish.

4. Was _____ pizza _____ than the _____?
No, it _____. It _____ more expensive than the milk.

get / gets – got – getting – gotten (отримувати)

Every week, I <u>get</u> milk from the supermarket.

He usually <u>gets</u> his vegetables at the market.

Last week, she <u>got</u> some drinks at the store.

They are <u>getting</u> some pizza for us right now.

We have never <u>gotten</u> ice cream together.

Part 4B: Verb Practice

1. Every day, we _____ lots of homework in our classes.
2. On Sundays, she _____ lots of work done at home.
3. Every week, he _____ food at the supermarket.
4. Last year, they _____ an expensive car.
5. Last weekend, I _____ a black hat at the store.
6. Earlier today, he _____ a good idea for his project.
7. Right now, she is _____ some drinks for the party.
8. We are _____ a new ball at the department store.
9. He has never _____ bread from that shop before.
10. You have _____ much taller in the past year.

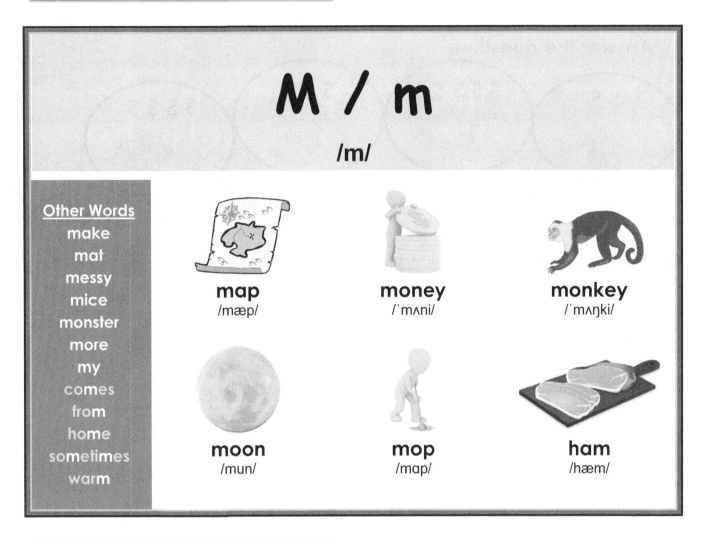

M / m

/m/

Other Words
make
mat
messy
mice
monster
more
my
comes
from
home
sometimes
warm

map
/mæp/

money
/ˈmʌni/

monkey
/ˈmʌŋki/

moon
/mun/

mop
/map/

ham
/hæm/

1. __y __onster __onkey __ops __essy __ats.

2. __oon __aps __ake __ice __ore __oney.

3. So__eti__es, war__ ha__ co__es fro__ ho__e.

Answer the questions

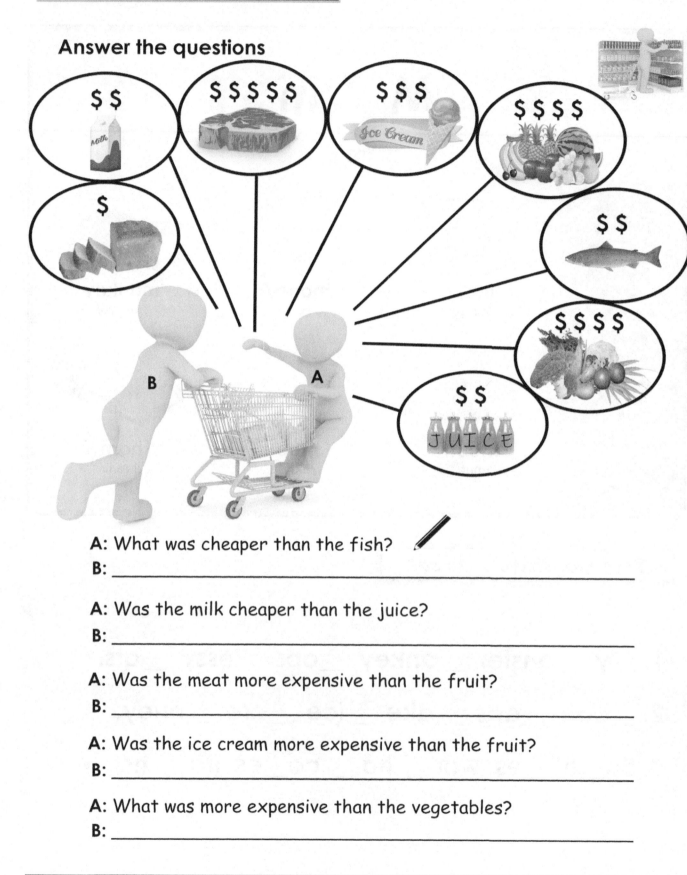

A: What was cheaper than the fish?

B: _____

A: Was the milk cheaper than the juice?

B: _____

A: Was the meat more expensive than the fruit?

B: _____

A: Was the ice cream more expensive than the fruit?

B: _____

A: What was more expensive than the vegetables?

B: _____

Lesson 29 Music

музика

Part 1A: Learn the words

1. **beautifully**
   красиво
2. **quietly**
   тихо
3. **slowly**
   повільно
4. **gracefully**
   витончено
5. **well**
   добре

6. **loudly**
   гучно
7. **quickly**
   швидко
8. **terribly**
   жахливо
9. **correctly**
   правильно
10. **badly**
    погано

 Practice speaking: "швидко " is "_quickly_" in English!

Part 1B: Write the words

Write the missing letters!   Write x 1   Write x 2

1. b__d__y
2. __e__u__i__u__l__
3. c__r__e__t__y
4. __r__c__f__l__y
5. l__u__l__
6. __u__c__l__
7. q__i__t__y
8. __l__w__y
9. t__r__i__l__
10. __e__l

179

How were you <u>playing the drums</u>?

✓ **I was** playing the drums **<u>quickly</u>**.

How was he <u>singing the song</u>?

✓ **He was** singing the song **<u>terribly</u>**.

 Winner's Tip! Learn: singing the song, playing the cello / drums / guitar / piano / violin

Part 2B: Fill in the blanks

1. How _____ he _____ the _____?
   _____ was playing the violin _____.

2. _____ was _____ playing the _____?
   She _____ playing _____ cello beautifully.

3. _____ _____ you playing the _____?
   _____ _____ playing the drums _____.

4. How _____ they _____ the guitar?
   _____ _____ playing the _____ _____.

Were you <u>playing the piano</u> <u>quietly</u>?

✓ **Yes, I was. I was** playing the piano quietly.
✗ **No, I wasn't. I wasn't** playing the piano quietly.

Was she <u>playing the guitar</u> <u>correctly</u>?

✓ **Yes, she was. She was** playing the guitar correctly.
✗ **No, she wasn't. She wasn't** playing the guitar correctly.

 Winner's Tip! Many adverbs end with "-ly"

Part 3B: Fill in the blanks

1. _____ _____ playing the _____ _____?
   Yes, I _____. I was _____ the drums correctly.

2. _____ _____ singing the _____ quietly?
   No, she wasn't. She _____ singing the song _____.

3. Were _____ _____ the piano _____?
   No, they _____. They weren't playing the _____ badly.

4. Was _____ playing the _____ _____?
   Yes, he _____. He _____ _____ the cello well.

notice / notices – noticed – noticing – noticed (помічати)

I never <u>notice</u> when he buys new clothes.

Every day, he <u>notices</u> who takes the bus.

Last week, she <u>noticed</u> we arrived late.

He is <u>noticing</u> many mistakes in our work.

She has never <u>noticed</u> our loud music.

Part 4B: Verb Practice

1. Each class, I _____ that the teacher speaks loudly.
2. On weekdays, she _____ what the students wear.
3. Every week, he _____ how the weather is hotter.
4. Last class, we _____ that he was writing slowly.
5. Last week, I _____ that the park had new trees.
6. Earlier today, he _____ that I wasn't feeling well.
7. Right now, she is _____ many changes in the city.
8. We are _____ big changes in the weather now.
9. He has never _____ that I always leave early.
10. They have _____ that the prices have increased.

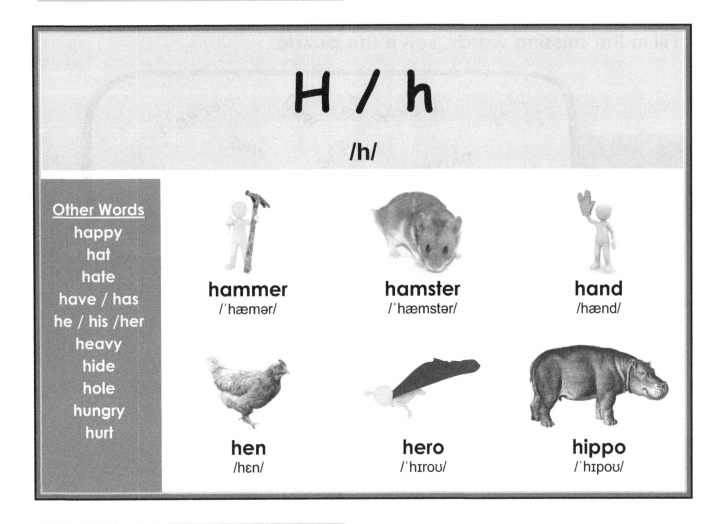

H / h
/h/

Other Words
happy
hat
hate
have / has
he / his /her
heavy
hide
hole
hungry
hurt

hammer
/ˈhæmər/

hamster
/ˈhæmstər/

hand
/hænd/

hen
/hɛn/

hero
/ˈhɪroʊ/

hippo
/ˈhɪpoʊ/

Part 5B: Write and read

1. __appy __amsters __ammer __eavy __ippos.

2. __eroes __ate __urting __ungry __ens.

3. __is __ands __ave __oles __iding __ats.

Fill in the missing words, solve the puzzle

♫ quickly he well weren't

the playing she was song

singing correctly was how playing ♫

1. __Was__ _____ playing _____ violin _____?
   (2)   (5)

2. No, they _____. They weren't _____
                                              (4)

   the _____ _____.
        (6)

3. Yes, _____ was. She was _____ the drums _____.
         (3)

4. _____ _____ he _____ the guitar?
    (1)

_____ __was__ _____ _____ _____ _____?
(1)   (2)   (3)   (4)   (5)   (6)

You: _____

Lesson 30 Jobs

профессії

Part 1A: Learn the words

1. **doctor**
   лікар
2. **cook**
   повар
3. **nurse**
   медсестра
4. **police officer**
   поліцейський
5. **taxi driver**
   таксист

6. **teacher**
   вчитель
7. **farmer**
   фермер
8. **salesclerk**
   продавець
9. **firefighter**
   пожежник
10. **builder**
    будівельник

 Practice speaking: "вчитель" means "<u>teacher</u>"!

Part 1B: Write the words

Write the missing letters!   Write x 1   Write x 2

1. b__i__d__r   _____   _____
2. __o__k   _____   _____
3. d__c__o__   _____   _____
4. __a__m__r   _____   _____
5. f__r__f__g__t__r   _____   _____
6. __u__s__   _____   _____
7. p__l__c__ o__f__c__r   _____   _____
8. __a__e__c__e__k   _____   _____
9. t__x__ d__i__e__   _____   _____
10. __e__c__e__   _____   _____

What job will you be working at <u>next year</u>?

✓ **Next year, I'll be working as a <u>salesclerk</u>.**
✗ **Next year, I won't be working as a <u>nurse</u>.**

What job will he be working at <u>in the future</u>?

✓ **In the future, he'll be working as a <u>doctor</u>.**
✗ **In the future, he won't be working as a <u>police officer</u>.**

Winner's Tip! Use: next year, next week, in the future

1. what _____ will she be _____ at next _____?
   _____ week, _____ be working as a salesclerk.

2. _____ job will _____ be working at in the future?
   In the _____, I won't be _____ as a _____.

3. _____ job will he be _____ at next _____?
   _____ year, _____ be _____ as a _____.

4. what _____ will he be _____ at _____ week?
   Next _____, _____ won't be working as a _____.

Will you be working as a <u>cook</u> <u>next week</u>?

✓ **Yes, I will be. I will be working as a** cook next week.
✗ **No, I won't be. I won't be working as a** cook next week.

Will she be working as a <u>farmer</u> <u>in the future</u>?

✓ **Yes, she will be. She will be working as a** farmer then.
✗ **No, she won't be. She won't be working as a** farmer then.

 Winner's Tip! Answer with "then" for time

Part 3B: Fill in the blanks

1. _____ he be _____ as a _____ next month?
   Yes, he will be. He will be _____ as a salesclerk _____.

2. Will _____ be working as a _____ _____?
   No, she won't be. She _____ be working as a teacher then.

3. Will _____ be working as a _____ in the future?
   Yes, I will be. I _____ be working as a builder _____.

4. _____ he be _____ as a _____ _____?
   No, he _____ be. He won't be _____ as a nurse then.

work / works – worked – working – worked (працювати)

Every evening, I <u>work</u> on my new computer.

She always <u>works</u> very early on Mondays.

Yesterday, we <u>worked</u> hard in the kitchen.

He is <u>working</u> as a doctor in the hospital.

You have never <u>worked</u> in another country.

Part 4B: Verb Practice

1. Every day, I _____ for many hours without a rest.

2. Each Monday, she _____ very late at the hospital.

3. Every week, he _____ in a different city.

4. Last night, we _____ on our science class project.

5. Last month, I _____ a lot at my part time job.

6. When he was younger, he _____ as a firefighter.

7. Right now, he is _____ as a cook at that place.

8. I am _____ on my English homework right now.

9. He has never _____ as a police officer before.

10. I have _____ very hard on my speech already.

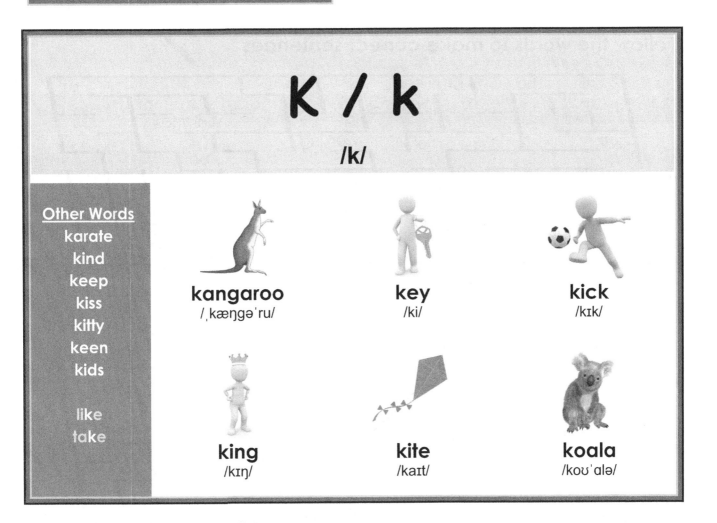

K / k

/k/

Other Words
karate
kind
keep
kiss
kitty
keen
kids

like
take

kangaroo
/ˌkæŋɡəˈru/

key
/ki/

kick
/kɪk/

king
/kɪŋ/

kite
/kaɪt/

koala
/koʊˈalə/

Part 5B: Write and read

1. __arate __angaroos li__e to __ick __ites.

2. __ind __ings __eep and __iss __itties.

3. __een __ids ta__e __eys and __oalas.

Follow the words to make correct sentences

1. What _____

Answer: _____ [rensu]

1. What _____

Answer: _____ [okco]

Unscramble the words and match

[ghrieefftir] [tocrdo] [rrafem] [eharect]

1. _____ **2.** _____ **3.** _____ **4.** _____

Write the correct answer next to the letter "A"

A: ___ **1.** Every time he _____ to the supermarket, he _____ fruit.
a) going / getting   **b)** go / get
c) goes / gets   **d)** went / gotten

A: ___ **2.** _____ class, the documentary movie _____ us about history.
a) Last / taught   **b)** Early / teach
c) This / teaching   **d)** Every / teached

A: ___ **3.** No, I _____. I wasn't _____ the tape measure to fix the shower.
a) was not / use   **b)** wasn't / using
c) haven't / uses   **d)** didn't / used

A: ___ **4.** _____ was he playing the piano? He was playing the piano _____.
a) Where / school   **b)** When / morning
c) How / good   **d)** How / well

A: ___ **5.** _____, you _____ be working as a doctor.
a) In next year / will   **b)** In the future / won't
c) Next week / haven't   **d)** In future / will

A: ___ **6.** The _____ were _____ than the drinks.
a) vegetable / more expensive   **b)** vegetables / more cheaper
c) vegetables / more expensive   **d)** vegetable / cheaper

A: ___ **7.** She felt _____ the sci-fi movie _____ violent.
a) this / was   **b)** these / was not
c) those / weren't   **d)** that / wasn't

A: ___ **8.** She _____ using the electric drill to _____ the bookshelf.
a) was / fix   **b)** will / fix
c) wasn't / fixed   **d)** is / fixing

A: ___ **9.** I _____ never _____ how quickly he plays guitar.
a) am / noticed   **b)** can / noticing
c) will / notices   **d)** have / noticed

A: ___ 10. Yes, she will _____. She will be working _____ a cook then.
a) be / at   **b)** be / as
c) work / for   **d)** working / at

A: ___ 11. Every weekend, he _____ his toolbox to _____ around the house.
a) using / working   **b)** uses / work
c) used / worked   **d)** uses / works

A: ___ 12. Did you feel that the action movie was enjoyable?
    Yes, I _____. I _____ that it was enjoyable.
a) feel / feel   **b)** was / felt
c) did / felt   **d)** had / feel

A: ___ 13. No, it _____. It wasn't _____ than the ice cream.
a) doesn't / more cheap   **b)** weren't / cheaper
c) wasn't / cheaper   **d)** wasn't / expensive

A: ___ 14. Was _____ playing the violin _____?
a) she / beautifully   **b)** he / terrible
c) you / correct   **d)** I / graceful

A: ___ 15. My brother _____ _____ as a firefighter for many years.
a) is / work   **b)** does / work
c) have / worked   **d)** has / worked

A: ___ 16. How did he _____ about the horror movie?
    He felt _____ it was scary.
a) feel / that   **b)** feeling / there
c) felt / there   **d)** feels / that

A: ___ 17. My sister _____ at the school _____ the cinema.
a) teach / by   **b)** teaching / across from
c) taught / between   **d)** teaches / near

A: ___ 18. _____ the drinks more expensive _____ the pizzas?
a) Where / than   **b)** Are / that
c) Was / than   **d)** Were / than

Answers on page 257

Lesson 31 Chores

хатня робота

Part 1A: Learn the words

1. **clean** the bedroom
   прибирати в спальні
2. **cook** dinner
   готувати обід
3. **do** the laundry
   прати
4. **feed** the pets
   годувати домашніх тварин
5. **iron** the clothes
   прасувати одяг

6. **make** the beds
   заправляти постіль
7. **mop** the floor
   мити підлогу
8. **take out** the trash
   виносити сміття
9. **vacuum** the carpet
   пилососити килим
10. **wash** the dishes
    мити посуд

 Practice speaking: "готувати обід " is "_cook dinner_" in English!

Part 1B: Write the words

Write the missing letters!   Write x 1   Write x 2

1. clean the __e__r__om _____   _____
2. cook __i__n__r   _____   _____
3. do the l__u__d__y   _____   _____
4. feed the __e__s   _____   _____
5. iron the c__o__h__s   _____   _____
6. make the __e__s   _____   _____
7. mop the f__o__r   _____   _____
8. take out the __r__s__ _____   _____
9. vacuum the c__r__e__   _____   _____
10. wash the __i__h__s   _____   _____

Which chores have you already finished?

✓ **I have already** <u>clean**ed** the bedroom</u>.

✗ **I haven't** <u>iron**ed** the clothes</u> **yet.**

Which chores has she already done?

✓ **She has already** <u>mop**ped** the floor</u>.

✗ **She hasn't** <u>cook**ed** dinner</u> **yet.**

 Winner's Tip! Learn: already, yet

1. what _____ has _____ _____ finished?
   He _____ done the laundry _____.

2. _____ chores _____ we already done?
   _____ have _____ washed the dishes.

3. _____ _____ have _____ already _____?
   I _____ _____ cooked dinner.

4. what _____ _____ she _____ _____?
   _____ hasn't mopped the floor _____.

Part 3A: Yes / No questions

Have you <u>wash</u>ed the dishes yet?

✓ **Yes, I have. I've already** washed **the dishes.**
✗ **No, I haven't. I haven't** washed **the dishes yet.**

Has he <u>done</u> the laundry yet?

✓ **Yes, he has. He has already** done **the laundry.**
✗ **No, he hasn't. He hasn't** done **the laundry yet.**

 Winner's Tip! Remember: have, haven't / has, hasn't

Part 3B: Fill in the blanks

1. Have _____ vacuumed the carpet _____?
   Yes, they _____. They've _____ vacuumed the carpet.

2. _____ you _____ yet?
   No, _____ haven't. I _____ ironed the clothes yet.

3. _____ _____ fed the pets _____?
   Yes, he _____. _____ has _____ fed the pets.

4. _____ _____ cleaned the bedroom _____?
   No, she _____. She _____ cleaned the bedroom yet.

know / knows – knew – knowing – known (знати)

I **know** how to do many different chores.

He **knows** how to cook a delicious lunch.

We **knew** that there was a lot of work to do.

Knowing how to speak well is important.*

She has never **known** where to buy fruit.

*gerund

Part 4B: Verb Practice

1. Usually, I _____ what I want to eat for dinner.
2. On Thursdays, he _____ he has a test at school.
3. She never _____ about problems in other countries.
4. Yesterday, we _____ the correct way to get there.
5. Last week, I _____ all the answers on the exam.
6. Last time, he _____ the best way to feed the dog.
7. _____ other languages is very useful and fun.
8. _____ how to cook is an important life skill.
9. He has never _____ how to do laundry or clean up.
10. They have _____ each other for many years.

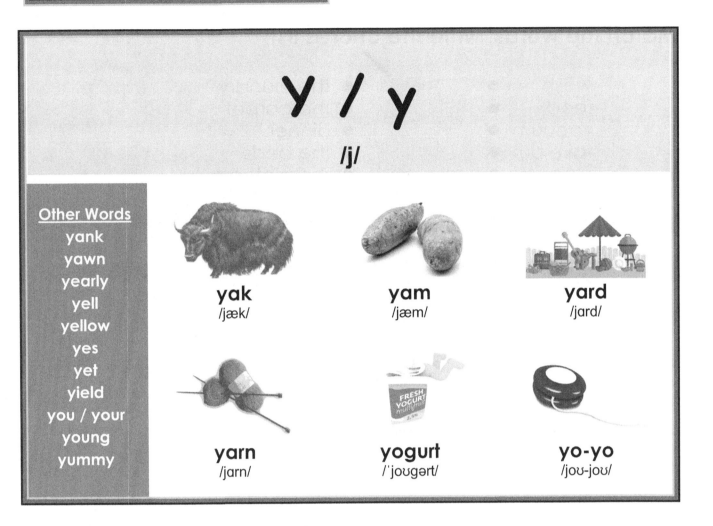

Y / y
/j/

Other Words
yank
yawn
yearly
yell
yellow
yes
yet
yield
you / your
young
yummy

yak
/jæk/

yam
/jæm/

yard
/jɑrd/

yarn
/jɑrn/

yogurt
/ˈjoʊɡərt/

yo-yo
/joʊ-joʊ/

Part 5B: Write and read

1. __ards __ield __early __ummy __ams.

2. __oung __arn __awns, __et __aks __ell "__ogurt".

3. __es, __ou usually __ank __our __ellow __o-__o.

Match the words, write the chores list

wash ●   ● the laundry
feed ●   ● the carpet
vacuum ●   ● dinner
take out ●   ● the beds
clean ●   ● the clothes
mop ●   ● the dishes
cook ●   ● the bedroom
do ●   ● the pets
iron ●   ● the floor
make ●   ● the trash

I've already...

1. _I've already washed the dishes._
2. _____
3. _____
4. _____
5. _____

He hasn't....yet.

1. _He hasn't_____
2. _____
3. _____
4. _____
5. _____

Lesson 32

Pets

домашні тварини

Part 1A: Learn the words

1. **dog**
   собака
2. **fish**
   рибка
3. **bird**
   пташка
4. **rabbit**
   кролик
5. **guinea pig**
   морська свинка

6. **cat**
   кіт
7. **turtle**
   черепаха
8. **mouse**
   мишка
9. **hamster**
   хом'як
10. **snake**
    змія

 Practice speaking: "кіт " is "_cat_" in English!

Part 1B: Write the words

Write the missing letters!   Write x 1   Write x 2

1. b__r__   _____   _____
2. __a__   _____   _____
3. __o__   _____   _____
4. f__s__   _____   _____
5. g__i__e__ p__g   _____   _____
6. __a__s__e__   _____   _____
7. m__u__e   _____   _____
8. __a__b__t   _____   _____
9. s__a__e   _____   _____
10. __u__t__e   _____   _____

199

Part 2A: Ask a question

What kind of pet have you had before?

✓ **I've had a <u>hamster</u>, but I've never had a <u>guinea pig</u>.**

What kind of pet has she owned before?

✓ **She's owned a <u>rabbit</u>, but she's never owned a <u>cat</u>.**

 Winner's Tip! he's / she's = he has / she has
Use verbs: had, owned

Part 2B: Fill in the blanks

1. What _____ of pet _____ he owned _____?
   He's _____ a bird, but _____ never owned a snake.

2. _____ kind of _____ has she _____ before?
   She's had a _____, but she's _____ had a mouse.

3. _____ kind of pet _____ they _____ before?
   _____ had a bird, _____ they've never had a cat.

4. What _____ of pet _____ you _____ before?
   I've owned a _____, but I've never _____ a dog.

200

Part 3A: Yes / No questions

Have you ever had a <u>fish</u>?

✓ Yes, I have. I've had a fish before.

✗ No, I haven't. I've never had a fish before.

Has he ever owned a <u>dog</u>?

✓ Yes, he has. He's owned a dog before.

✗ No, he hasn't. He's never owned a dog before.

⭐ **Winner's Tip!** Use: "before"

Part 3B: Fill in the blanks

1. _____ they _____ had a _____?
   No, they _____. They've _____ had a snake before.

2. _____ she ever _____ a _____?
   No, she _____. She's _____ owned a bird _____.

3. Have _____ _____ owned a _____?
   _____, I have. _____ _____ a cat before.

4. _____ he _____ _____ a _____?
   Yes, he _____. _____ had a rabbit _____.

Part 4A: Verb of the day

feed / feeds – fed – feeding – fed (годувати)

Early every morning, I <u>feed</u> my pet turtles.

She <u>feeds</u> her rabbits and dogs daily.

Last Tuesday, he <u>fed</u> his baby some fruit.

He is <u>feeding</u> some milk to a cat now.

They have never <u>fed</u> any tigers or lions.

Part 4B: Verb Practice

1. Every afternoon, I _____ my fish a lot of food.

2. On Thursdays, she _____ the cats near her house.

3. Every weekend, he _____ his neighbor's pet dog.

4. Last year, we _____ our young baby a lot less milk.

5. Last week, I _____ my friend's new pet turtle.

6. Earlier today, they _____ the birds in the park.

7. Right now, she is _____ her kids some healthy food.

8. We are _____ too much junk food to kids in schools.

9. He has never _____ a guinea pig or mouse before.

10. I have _____ many different types of pets before.

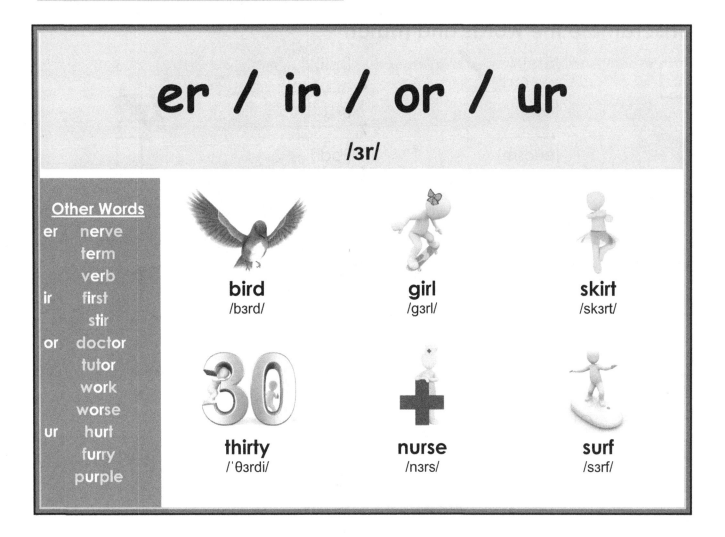

er / ir / or / ur

/ɜr/

Other Words

er   nerve
       term
       verb
ir   first
       stir
or   doctor
       tutor
       work
       worse
ur   hurt
       furry
       purple

bird /bɜrd/

girl /gɜrl/

skirt /skɜrt/

thirty /ˈθɜrdi/

nurse /nɜrs/

surf /sɜrf/

1. G___l doct___s h___t n___se n___ves w___se.

2. H___ f___st tut___ w___ks th___ty v___b t___ms.

3. F___ry sk___ts st___ p___ple s___f b___ds.

Part 6: Fun review

Unscramble the words and match

[atc]
1. ___cat___

[lertut]
2. _____

[euosm]
3. _____

[eramhst]
4. _____

[kasne]
5. _____

[hsfi]
6. _____

[ogd]
7. _____

[ibdr]
8. _____

[tiabbr]
9. _____

[nuiage igp]
10. _____

Have, has, or had? 've or 's? Complete the sentences

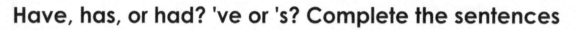

A: What kind of pet __has__ he __had__ before?

B: He_'s___ _____ a [cat]¹, but he_____ never _____ a [ ]².

A: What kind of pet _____ you _____ before?

B: I_____ _____ a [ ]³, but I_____ never _____ a [ ]⁴.

A: _____ you ever _____ a [ ]⁹?

B: Yes, I _____. I_____ _____ a [ ] before.

A: _____ she ever _____ a [ ]⁵?

B: Yes, she _____. She_____ _____ a [ ] before.

Lesson 33 Martial arts

бойові мистецтва

Part 1A: Learn the words

1. **karate**
   карате
2. **taekwondo**
   тхеквондо
3. **kung fu**
   кунг фу
4. **judo**
   дзюдо
5. **boxing**
   бокс

6. **kendo**
   кендо
7. **tai chi**
   тай чі
8. **sumo**
   сумо
9. **kickboxing**
   кікбоксинг
10. **fencing**
    фехтування

 Practice speaking: "фехтування" is "_fencing_" in English!

Part 1B: Write the words

Write the missing letters!   Write x 1   Write x 2

1. b__x__n__   _____   _____
2. __e__c__n__   _____   _____
3. j__d__   _____   _____
4. __a__a__e   _____   _____
5. k__n__o   _____   _____
6. __i__k__o__i__g   _____   _____
7. k__n__ f__   _____   _____
8. __u__o   _____   _____
9. t__e__w__n__o   _____   _____
10. __a__ c__i   _____   _____

Which martial arts have you learned before?

✓ **I've learned <u>karate</u>, but I've never learned <u>tai chi</u>.**

Which martial arts has he tried before?

✓ **He's tried <u>boxing</u>, but he's never tried <u>sumo</u>.**

 Winner's Tip! he's = he has / she's = she has
Use verbs: done, learned, studied, tried

Part 2B: Fill in the blanks

1. which _____ arts _____ she _____ before?
_____ done judo, but she's _____ done taekwondo.

2. _____ martial _____ have _____ tried before?
They've tried _____, but _____ never tried karate.

3. which _____ arts _____ you _____ before?
_____ learned kung fu, but I've never learned _____.

4. _____ martial _____ has he studied _____?
He's _____ _____, but he's never _____ kendo.

Have you ever studied <u>taekwondo</u>?

✓ **Yes, I have. I've studied** taekwondo **since I was nine.**
✗ **No, I haven't. I've never studied** taekwondo **before.**

Has she ever done <u>kung fu</u>?

✓ **Yes, she has. She's done** kung fu **for five years.**
✗ **No, she hasn't. She's never done** kung fu **before.**

 Winner's Tip! Learn: for, since, never

Part 3B: Fill in the blanks

1. _____ you _____ learned karate?
   Yes, I _____. I've _____ _____ for two years.

2. Has _____ ever _____ _____?
   No, _____ hasn't. She's _____ done judo before.

3. _____ they _____ done _____?
   Yes, _____ have. _____ done taekwondo for six years.

4. _____ he ever _____ _____?
   Yes, he _____. He's studied tai chi _____ he was ten.

kick / kicks – kicked – kicking – kicked (ударяти ногою)

Every taekwondo class, we <u>kick</u> the pads.

He <u>kicks</u> the ball quite well every game.

Last night at karate, I <u>kicked</u> the teacher.

She is <u>kicking</u> in kung fu class right now.

He has never <u>kicked</u> another person.

Part 4B: Verb Practice

1. Every weekend, I _____ the ball with my brother.

2. In taekwondo class, he often _____ very high.

3. Every time she's angry, she _____ the door closed.

4. Last karate class, he _____ his friend's leg hard.

5. Last week, the horse _____ him in the stomach.

6. Earlier today, we _____ a lot while swimming.

7. He is _____ his legs like a frog in the pool.

8. They are _____ the football outside right now.

9. She has never _____ anyone very hard before.

10. We have already _____ that ball so many times.

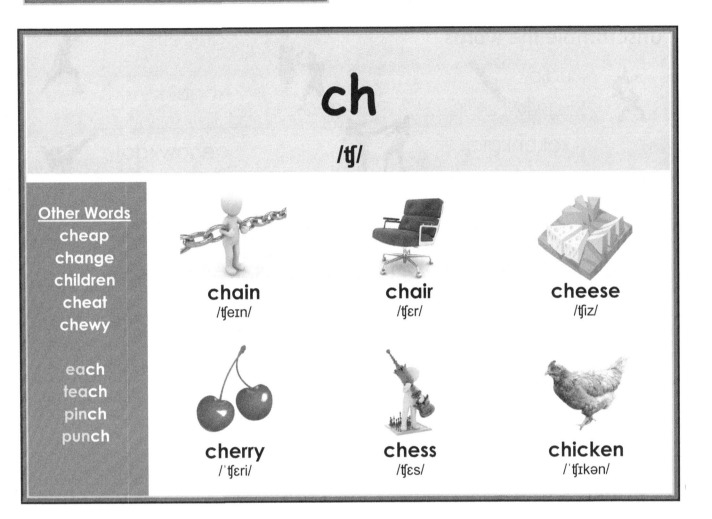

ch
/tʃ/

Other Words
cheap
change
children
cheat
chewy

each
teach
pinch
punch

chain
/tʃeɪn/

chair
/tʃɛr/

cheese
/tʃiz/

cherry
/ˈtʃɛri/

chess
/tʃɛs/

chicken
/ˈtʃɪkən/

Part 5B: Write and read

1. Ea___ ___eap ___eese ___anges ___ildren.

2. Pun___ed ___ickens tea___ ___ess ___eating.

3. ___ained ___airs pin___ ___ewy ___erries.

Unscramble the words

udjo 
judo

xokbnkgici
_____

oendk
_____

gnicefn
_____

xbgoin
_____

aenowkdot
_____

ugkn uf
_____

Unscramble and complete the conversation

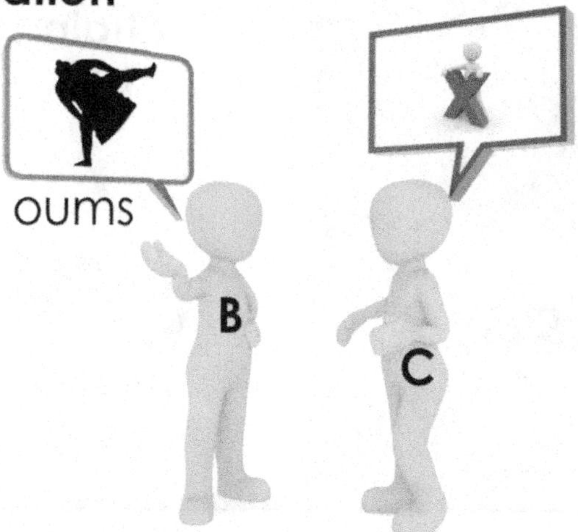

B: Have you ever tried _____?

    C: No, _____

    _____.

oums

B

C

ita hci

D E

D: Have you ever learned _____?

    E: Yes, _____

    _____.

aartke

F

F: Have you ever studied _____?

    You: _____

    _____.

Lesson 34 In the kitchen

на кухні

Part 1A: Learn the words

1. **refrigerator**
   холодильник
2. **coffee maker**
   кавоварка
3. **microwave oven**
   мікрохвильова піч
4. **stove**
   піч
5. **blender**
   блендер

6. **cupboard**
   шафа
7. **rice cooker**
   рисоварка
8. **dish rack**
   стійка для посуду
9. **pan**
   каструля
10. **toaster**
    тостер

 Practice speaking: "тостер" is "_toaster_" in English!

Part 1B: Write the words

Write the missing letters!   Write x 1   Write x 2

1. b _ e _ d _ r   _____   _____
2. _ o _ f _ e m _ k _ r   _____   _____
3. c _ p _ o _ r _   _____   _____
4. _ i _ h r _ c _   _____   _____
5. mi _ ro _ a _ e o _ en   _____   _____
6. _ a _   _____   _____
7. r _ f _ i _ e _ a _ o _   _____   _____
8. _ i _ e c _ o _ e _   _____   _____
9. s _ o _ e   _____   _____
10. _ o _ s _ e _   _____   _____

211

What do you have to clean <u>later</u>?

✓ **Later, I have to clean the <u>toaster</u>.**

✗ **Later, I don't have to clean the <u>stove</u>.**

What does he have to clean <u>tonight</u>?

✓ **Tonight, he has to clean the <u>microwave oven</u>.**

✗ **Tonight, he doesn't have to clean the <u>rice cooker</u>.**

 Winner's Tip! Use future times: later, tonight, tomorrow, etc.

Part 2B: Fill in the blanks

1. what _____ she _____ to clean _____?
   Tomorrow, _____ has to _____ the blender.

2. _____ do _____ have to _____ tonight?
   _____, they don't _____ to clean _____ stove.

3. what _____ we _____ to clean _____?
   Later, we don't have to _____ the _____.

4. _____ does _____ have to clean _____?
   Tomorrow, he _____ to clean _____ cupboard.

Do you have to clean the <u>cupboard</u> <u>tomorrow</u>?

✓ **Yes, I do. I have to clean the cupboard tomorrow.**

✗ **No, I don't. I don't have to clean it tomorrow.**

Does she have to clean the <u>pan</u> <u>later</u>?

✓ **Yes, she does. She has to clean the pan later.**

✗ **No, she doesn't. She doesn't have to clean it later.**

 Winner's Tip! Learn: "have to / has to"

Part 3B: Fill in the blanks

1. Do _____ have to _____ the cupboard _____?
   _____, we _____. We have to clean it tonight.

2. _____ she _____ to clean the dish rack _____?
   No, _____ doesn't. She _____ have to clean it later.

3. Do _____ have to _____ the toaster _____?
   Yes, I do. I _____ to clean _____ tomorrow.

4. Does _____ have to clean the _____ next week?
   Yes, he _____. He _____ to _____ it next week.

clean / cleans – cleaned – cleaning – cleaned (чистити, прибирати)

Every weekend, I <u>clean</u> my kitchen well.

She usually <u>cleans</u> the toaster and stove.

They <u>cleaned</u> the classroom very quickly.

He is <u>cleaning</u> the swimming pool now.

That beach has been <u>cleaned</u> many times.

Part 4B: Verb Practice

1. Every morning, I _____ the sink in the bathroom.
2. On weekends, she _____ the coffee maker well.
3. Every month, he _____ the whole refrigerator.
4. Last time, we _____ the entire yard and garage.
5. Yesterday, I _____ the stove after cooking lunch.
6. This morning, he _____ his tools in the toolbox.
7. Right now, she is _____ the vegetables for dinner.
8. I am _____ his teddy bear that fell on the ground.
9. He has never _____ his microwave oven before.
10. We have _____ the rice cooker many times already.

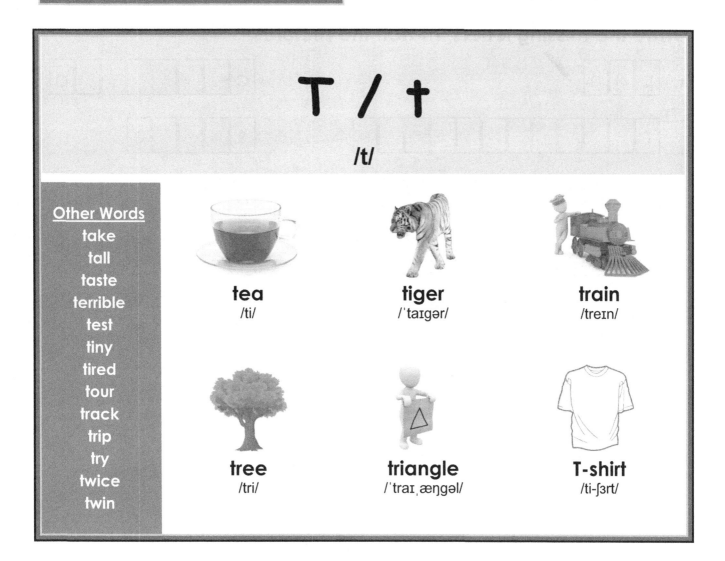

T / t

/t/

Other Words
take
tall
taste
terrible
test
tiny
tired
tour
track
trip
try
twice
twin

tea
/ti/

tiger
/ˈtaɪgər/

train
/treɪn/

tree
/tri/

triangle
/ˈtraɪˌæŋgəl/

T-shirt
/ti-ʃɜrt/

Part 5B: Write and read

1. __our __rains __ake __es__ __rack __rips __wice.

2. __en __iny __ired __igers __ry __riangle __-shir__s.

3. __wo __all __win __rees __as__e __errible __ea.

Part 6: Fun review

Write the missing letters, match the pictures

```
E [p][a][n]  ✎               c [ ][ ][ ][ ][ ] d
     3                             6

  r [ ][ ][ ][ ][ ][ ][ ][ ][ ] r    s [ ][ ][e]
       15        4                      9

  c [ ][ ][ ]  [ ][ ][ ] r        b [ ][ ][ ][ ] r
       7        14                   11  12  5

  m [ ][ ][ ][ ][ ][ ]  [ ][ ] n    t [ ][ ][ ][ ] r
      13    1                          8

  r [ ][ ]  [ ][ ][ ][ ] r        d [ ][ ]  [ ][ ] k
          10                          2
```

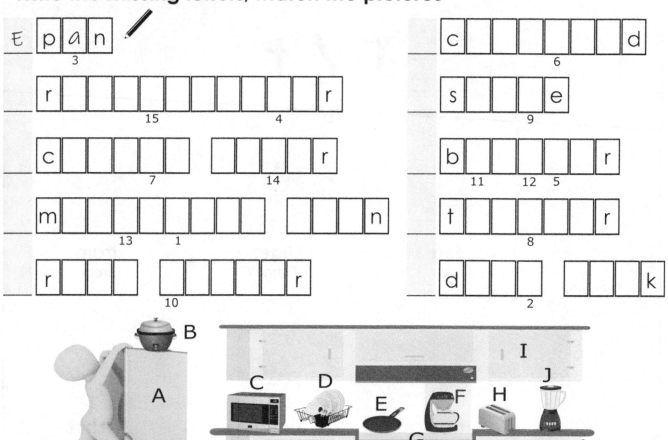

Use the numbers above to write the words

```
[ ][ ][a][ ]  [ ][ ][ ][ ]  [ ][ ]  [ ][ ][ ][ ]  [ ][ ]  [ ][ ][ ][ ][ ]
 1  2  3  4    5  6  7  8    2  7    2  3  9  7    4  6    10 11 7  3  12

[ ][ ][ ][ ][ ] ?
11 3  4  7 13

[ ][ ][ ][ ][ ] , [ ][ ]  [ ][ ][ ]  [ ][ ]  [ ][ ][ ][ ][ ]  [ ][ ][ ]
11 3  4  7 13     2  7    2  3  8    4  6    10 11 7  3  12    4  2  7

[ ][ ][ ][ ][ ][ ][ ] .
14 15 4 10  2  7 12
```

216

Lesson 35 Fast food

фастфуд

Part 1A: Learn the words

1. **doughnut**
   пончик
2. **cheeseburger**
   Чізбургер
3. **chicken nuggets**
   курячі нагетси
4. **pancake**
   млинець
5. **taco**
   тако

6. **french fries**
   картопля фрі
7. **onion rings**
   цибулеві кільця
8. **hot dog**
   хот дог
9. **fried chicken**
   смажена курка
10. **burrito**
   буріто

 Practice speaking: "смажена курка " is "_fried chicken_" in English!

Part 1B: Write the words

Write the missing letters!   Write x 1   Write x 2

1. b__r__i__o   _____   _____
2. __h_e__e__u_g__r   _____   _____
3. c__i__k__n n__gg__ts   _____   _____
4. __o__g__n__t__   _____   _____
5. f__e__c__ f__i__s   _____   _____
6. __r_e__ __h_c_e__   _____   _____
7. h__t __o__   _____   _____
8. __n__o__ r__n__s   _____   _____
9. p__n__a__e   _____   _____
10. __a__o   _____   _____

Part 2A: Ask a question

Would you prefer the <u>cheeseburger</u> or the <u>burrito</u>?

✓ **I would prefer the burrito to the cheeseburger.**

Would she prefer the <u>pancake</u> or the <u>doughnut</u>?

✓ **She would prefer the pancake to the doughnut.**

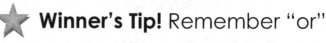 **Winner's Tip!** Remember "or"

Part 2B: Fill in the blanks

1. Would he _____ the _____ or the chicken nuggets?
   He _____ prefer the _____ to the burrito.

2. _____ you prefer _____ taco or the _____?
   _____ would prefer the _____ to the hot dog.

3. Would _____ prefer the _____ to the french fries?
   They would _____ the french fries to the _____.

4. _____ she prefer the _____ or the onion rings?
   _____ would _____ the onion rings to the pancake.

Would you prefer the <u>hot dog</u> to the <u>onion rings</u>?

✓ **Yes, I would. I'd prefer the** hot dog.

✗ **No, I wouldn't. I wouldn't prefer the** hot dog.

Would he prefer the <u>taco</u> to the <u>fried chicken</u>?

✓ **Yes, he would. He'd prefer the** taco.

✗ **No, he wouldn't. He wouldn't prefer the** taco.

 Winner's Tip! I'd = I would / he'd = he would, etc.

Part 3B: Fill in the blanks

1. Would _____ prefer _____ burrito to the pancake?
_____, she would. _____ prefer the _____.

2. _____ you _____ the fried chicken to the hot dog?
No, I _____. I wouldn't _____ the _____.

3. Would _____ prefer the _____ to the doughnut?
Yes, they _____. _____ prefer _____ onion rings.

4. Would _____ prefer the _____ to the cheeseburger?
_____, he _____. _____ prefer _____ taco.

Part 4A: Verb of the day

try / tries – tried – trying – tried (пробувати)

Every vacation, I like to <u>try</u> new fast food.

She always <u>tries</u> to eat healthier meals.

They <u>tried</u> the fried chicken and loved it.

We are <u>trying</u> to decide what to eat later.

He has <u>tried</u> all the food at that restaurant.

Part 4B: Verb Practice

1. Every summer, I _____ traveling to a new place.
2. On weekends, he _____ different kinds of food.
3. Sometimes, she _____ cooking special food at home.
4. Last year, we _____ painting the room dark blue.
5. Last week, I _____ working at the supermarket.
6. Yesterday, she _____ a burrito for the first time.
7. Right now, he is _____ to earn a lot more money.
8. I am _____ to study, but it's very loud here.
9. She has never _____ eating fried chicken before.
10. I have _____ many different types of fast food.

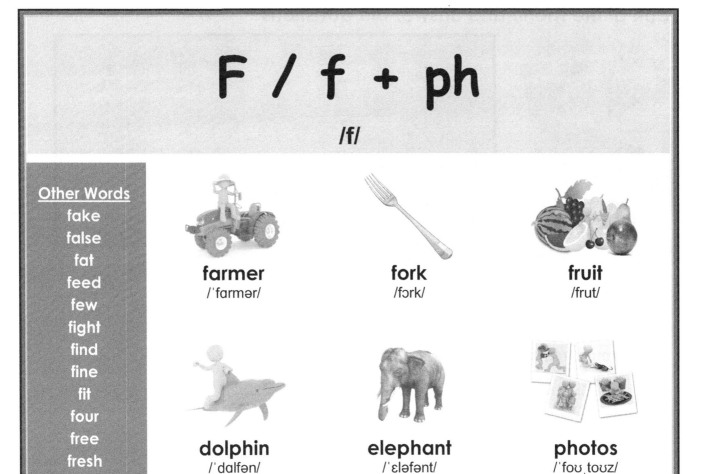

F / f + ph

/f/

Other Words
fake
false
fat
feed
few
fight
find
fine
fit
four
free
fresh
frog

farmer
/ˈfɑrmər/

fork
/fɔrk/

fruit
/frut/

dolphin
/ˈdɑlfən/

elephant
/ˈɛləfənt/

photos
/ˈfoʊˌtoʊz/

Part 5B: Write and read

1. __our __ine __orks __ind __ree __resh __ruit.

2. __ew __alse __armers __ake __eeding __rogs.

3. __it dol__ins __ight __at ele__ant __otos.

Look at the menu and answer the questions

Menu

- ↓ french fries
- ✗ onion rings
- ↓ doughnut
- ✗ pancake
- ✗ chicken nuggets
- ↓ hot dog
- ✗ taco
- ↓ fried chicken
- ↓ cheeseburger
- ✗ burrito

A: Would you prefer the doughnut **or** the pancake?

B: _I would prefer the doughnut to the pancake._

A: Would he prefer the french fries **or** the onion rings?

B: _____

A: Would he prefer the chicken nuggets **or** the hot dog?

B: _____

A: Would she prefer the taco **to** the fried chicken?

B: No, _____

A: Would he prefer the cheeseburger **to** the burrito?

B: _____

Write the correct answer next to the letter "A"

A: ___ **1.** Has he _____ the floor yet? Yes, he _____.
a) mop / mop   **b)** mopped / has
c) mopped / already   **d)** mopping / did

A: ___ **2.** _____ _____ a fish, but he's never owned a snake.
a) He'll / had   **b)** He / have
c) He's / owned   **d)** He's / having

A: ___ **3.** _____ tried kung fu, but _____ never tried boxing.
a) She'll / she won't   **b)** She'd / she
c) She / she'll   **d)** She's / she's

A: ___ **4.** Yes, she _____. She _____ to clean the rice cooker later.
a) cleans / must   **b)** does / has
c) has / have   **d)** is / having

A: ___ **5.** Last Sunday, _____ _____ eating at that new fast food restaurant.
a) we / try   **b)** she / tries
c) he / trying   **d)** they / tried

A: ___ **6.** Has he _____ had a bird? Yes, he _____. He's had a bird before.
a) ever / has   **b)** ever / had
c) since / had   **d)** never / owned

A: ___ **7.** Yes, I _____. I've _____ judo _____ I was five.
a) do / learned / for   **b)** have / studied / since
c) have / do / since   **d)** am / tried / for

A: ___ **8.** Tonight, he _____ have to _____ the refrigerator.
a) isn't / clean   **b)** doesn't / clean
c) hasn't / cleaning   **d)** doesn't / cleaning

A: ___ **9.** _____ you _____ the chicken nuggets or the cheeseburger?
a) Will / preferring   **b)** Can / prefer
c) Would / prefer   **d)** Do / preferring

A: ___ **10.** He hasn't _____ the beds _____.
a) make / yet   **b)** making / already
c) makes / already   **d)** made / yet

A: ___ **11.** Last Saturday, we _____ a _____ in the park.
a) fed / rabbit   **b)** feeding / bird
c) feeds / dog   **d)** feed / cat

A: ___ **12.** She already _____ how to _____ the carpet.
a) know / clean   **b)** knows / vacuum
c) knowing / do   **d)** knew / vacuuming

A: ___ **13.** Earlier today during the game, I _____ the ball many times.
a) kick   **b)** kicking
c) kicked   **d)** 've kicked

A: ___ **14.** They _____ the kitchen very _____.
a) cleans / bad   **b)** cleaning / terrible
c) are clean / quickly   **d)** cleaned / slowly

A: ___ **15.** Would he prefer the hot dog _____ the burrito?
              Yes, he would. _____ prefer the hot dog.
a) or / He'll   **b)** to / He's
c) to / He'd   **d)** or / He's

A: ___ **16.** What kind of pet have they _____ _____?
a) owned / before   **b)** had / ever
c) owning / already   **d)** having / before

A: ___ **17.** Yes, he _____. He's learned fencing _____ two years.
a) has / since   **b)** has / for
c) learned / along   **d)** does / since

A: ___ **18.** Does she _____ to clean the blender _____?
a) have / yesterday   **b)** has / later
c) have / tomorrow   **d)** having / tonight

Answers on page 257

Lesson 36

Hobbies

хобі

Part 1A: Learn the words

1. **do gardening**
   займатися садівництвом
2. **go hiking**
   відправлятися в піший похід
3. **take photographs**
   Фотографувати
4. **play video games**
   грати у відео ігри
5. **listen to music**
   слухати музику

6. **go camping**
   відправлятися в похід з палатками
7. **play chess**
   грати в шахи
8. **watch movies**
   дивитися фільми
9. **go fishing**
   рибалити
10. **sing karaoke**
    співати в караоке

 Practice speaking: "грати в шахи " means "play chess"!

Part 1B: Write the words

Write the missing letters!   Write x 1   Write x 2

1. do __a__d__n__n__   _____   _____
2. go c__m__i__g   _____   _____
3. go __i__h__n__   _____   _____
4. go h__k__n__   _____   _____
5. listen to __u__i__   _____   _____
6. play c__e__s   _____   _____
7. play v__d__o g__mes   _____   _____
8. sing __a__a__k__   _____   _____
9. take p__o__o__r__phs   _____   _____
10. watch __o__i__s   _____   _____

Part 2A: Ask a question

Why do you like to <u>play video games</u>?

✓ **I like to** play video games **because it's <u>exciting</u>.**

Why does he like to <u>go fishing</u>?

✓ **He likes to** go fishing **because it's <u>relaxing</u>.**

 Winner's Tip! Learn: fun, exciting, interesting, relaxing

Part 2B: Fill in the blanks

1. why _____ they _____ to go camping?
   _____ like to go camping _____ _____ relaxing.

2. _____ does _____ like to _____?
   She _____ to take photographs because it's _____.

3. why _____ you _____ to _____?
   I _____ to do gardening _____ it's interesting.

4. why _____ _____ like _____ listen to music?
   He _____ to _____ because it's _____.

Do you think <u>watching</u> <u>movies</u> is <u>interesting</u>?

✓ **Yes, I do. I think** watching movies **is** interesting.

✗ **No, I don't. I think** watching movies **is** <u>boring</u>.

Does he think <u>going</u> <u>hiking</u> is <u>fun</u>?

✓ **Yes, he does. He thinks going hiking is** fun.

✗ **No, he doesn't. He thinks going hiking is** <u>unexciting</u>.

 Winner's Tip! Learn: boring, unexciting, uninteresting

Part 3B: Fill in the blanks

1. Do _____ think singing karaoke is _____?
   Yes, I _____. I _____ singing karaoke is exciting.

2. _____ she _____ _____ is interesting?
   No, _____ doesn't. She _____ playing chess is boring.

3. Do _____ _____ playing video games is _____?
   Yes, _____ do. They _____ playing video games is fun.

4. Does _____ think _____ is relaxing?
   No, he _____. He _____ going camping is _____.

enjoy / enjoys – enjoyed – enjoying – enjoyed (насолоджуватися)

I always <u>enjoy</u> listening to music in my kitchen.

Every morning, he <u>enjoys</u> a cup of hot coffee.

They <u>enjoyed</u> hiking in the mountains together.

She is <u>enjoying</u> her newest video game.

We have <u>enjoyed</u> eating his cooking a lot.

Part 4B: Verb Practice

1. Every spring, I _____ doing gardening on hot days.

2. On Tuesdays, she _____ watching new movies.

3. Every month, he _____ getting paid at his job.

4. Last year, we _____ the great summer weather.

5. Last week, I _____ a camping trip with friends.

6. Yesterday, they _____ singing karaoke loudly.

7. Right now, he is _____ the new music he found.

8. They are _____ the photographs from their trip.

9. He has never _____ going hiking in the mountains.

10. We have _____ watching many movies together.

oi / oy

/ɔɪ/

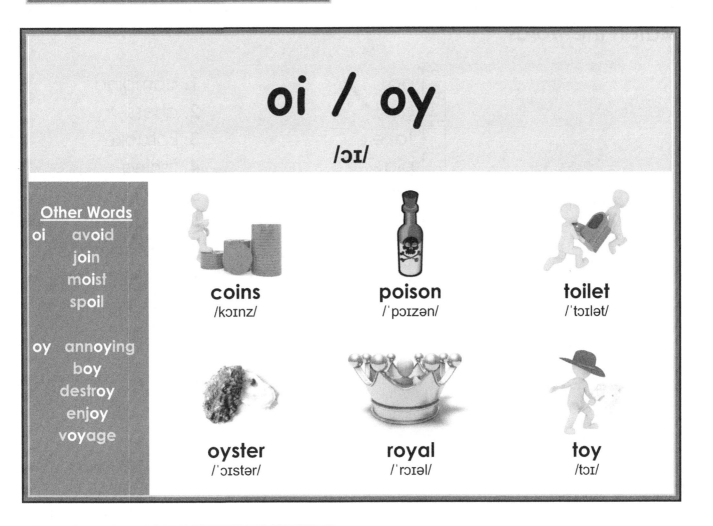

Other Words

oi   avoid
      join
      moist
      spoil

oy annoying
      boy
      destroy
      enjoy
      voyage

coins
/kɔɪnz/

poison
/ˈpɔɪzən/

toilet
/ˈtɔɪlət/

oyster
/ˈɔɪstər/

royal
/ˈrɔɪəl/

toy
/tɔɪ/

1. P___son ___sters av___d m___st t___lets.

2. R___al c___ns enj___ j___ning v___ages.

3. Sp___led ann___ing b___s destr___ t___s.

Part 6: Fun review

Match the words

- ☐ do
- ☐ 1 go
- ☐ take
- ☐ play
- ☐ listen to
- ☐ go
- ☐ play
- ☐ watch
- ☐ go
- ☐ sing

1. camping
2. chess
3. karaoke
4. fishing
5. movies
6. gardening
7. photographs
8. music
9. video games
10. hiking

Like or likes?

1. He __likes__ to __go camping__ because it's __fun__.
2. She _____ to _____ because it's _____.
3. They _____ to _____ because it's _____.
4. You _____ to _____ because it's _____.
5. We _____ to _____ because it's _____.

Unscramble the adjectives

[nuf]
[airgxlen]
[centigxi]
[eninirgestt]

[ngboir]
[nietingurstne]
[incunigtex]

Do, does, don't, or doesn't?

6. Yes, she __does__. She thinks __doing gardening__ is _____.
7. No, he _____. He thinks _____ is _____.
8. Yes, I _____. I think _____ is _____.
9. No, we _____. We think _____ is _____.
10. Yes, he _____. He thinks _____ is _____.

Lesson 37 In the living room

в вітальні

Part 1A: Learn the words

1. **bookcase**
   книжкова шафа
2. **television**
   телевізор
3. **clock**
   годинник
4. **coffee table**
   журнальний столик
5. **armchair**
   крісло

6. **painting**
   картина
7. **TV stand**
   підставка під телевізор
8. **rug**
   килим
9. **sofa**
   диван
10. **vase**
    ваза

 Practice speaking: "ваза " is "_vase_" in English!

Part 1B: Write the words

Write the missing letters!   Write x 1   Write x 2

1. _ r _ c _ a _ r   _____   _____
2. b _ o _ c _ s _   _____   _____
3. _ l _ c _   _____   _____
4. c _ f _ e _ t _ b _ e   _____   _____
5. _ a _ n _ i _ g   _____   _____
6. _ u _   _____   _____
7. s _ f _   _____   _____
8. _ e _ e _ i _ i _ n   _____   _____
9. T _ s _ a _ d   _____   _____
10. _ a _ e   _____   _____

What was as expensive as the <u>bookcase</u>?

✓ The <u>television</u> was as expensive as the bookcase.
✗ The <u>coffee table</u> wasn't as expensive as the bookcase.

What was as cheap as the <u>vase</u>?

✓ The <u>clock</u> was as cheap as the vase.
✗ The <u>TV stand</u> wasn't as cheap as the vase.

 **Winner's Tip!** Learn: as...as

1. what _____ as _____ as the _____?
   The rug wasn't _____ cheap _____ the coffee table.

2. _____ was _____ expensive as _____ sofa?
   _____ armchair wasn't as _____ as the _____.

3. what _____ _____ expensive as the _____?
   The TV stand was as _____ as _____ bookcase.

4. _____ _____ as _____ as the _____?
   _____ painting was _____ cheap as _____ vase.

Was the <u>sofa</u> as expensive as the <u>armchair</u>?

✓ **Yes, it was. It was just as expensive as the** armchair.
✗ **No, it wasn't. It wasn't as expensive as the** armchair.

Were the <u>paintings</u> as cheap as the <u>rugs</u>?

✓ **Yes, they were. They were just as cheap as the** rugs.
✗ **No, they weren't. They weren't as cheap as the** rugs.

 **Winner's Tip!** Learn: "just"

Part 3B: Fill in the blanks

1. Was the clock _____ expensive as the _____?
   No, it _____. It wasn't as _____ as the television.

2. _____ the TV stand as _____ as the _____?
   No, _____ wasn't. It _____ as cheap as the bookcase.

3. _____ the _____ as expensive as _____ sofa?
   Yes, it was. It was _____ as _____ as the _____.

4. Was _____ rug as _____ as the _____?
   Yes, it was. It _____ just _____ cheap as the painting.

Part 4A: Verb of the day

move / moves – moved – moving – moved (рухатися)

I always <u>move</u> my sofa around the room.

Every year, he <u>moves</u> to a new house.

She <u>moved</u> to Australia alone last year.

We are <u>moving</u> the bookcase downstairs.

He has <u>moved</u> many times recently.

Part 4B: Verb Practice

1. I often _____ all of the armchairs in my living room.
2. Every year, she _____ to a different house.
3. After each class, he _____ his books to a new place.
4. Yesterday, they _____ the sofa into another room.
5. Last Thursday, I _____ my favorite painting.
6. Last night, someone _____ my food in the kitchen.
7. Right now, he is _____ the rug into his bedroom.
8. We are _____ the heavy coffee table right now.
9. She has never _____ her old bookcase before.
10. They have _____ most of the furniture already.

qu
/kw/

Other Words
quack
quarter
quick
quietly
quit
quite
quiz
quote

equal

quail
/kweɪl/

queen
/kwin/

question
/ˈkwɛstʃən/

quilt
/kwɪlt/

square
/skwɛr/

squirrel
/ˈskwərəl/

1. ___eens ___estion e___al s___are ___ilts.

2. ___arter ___ails ___ack ___ite ___ietly.

3. ___ick s___irrels ___it ___oting ___izzes.

Answer the questions

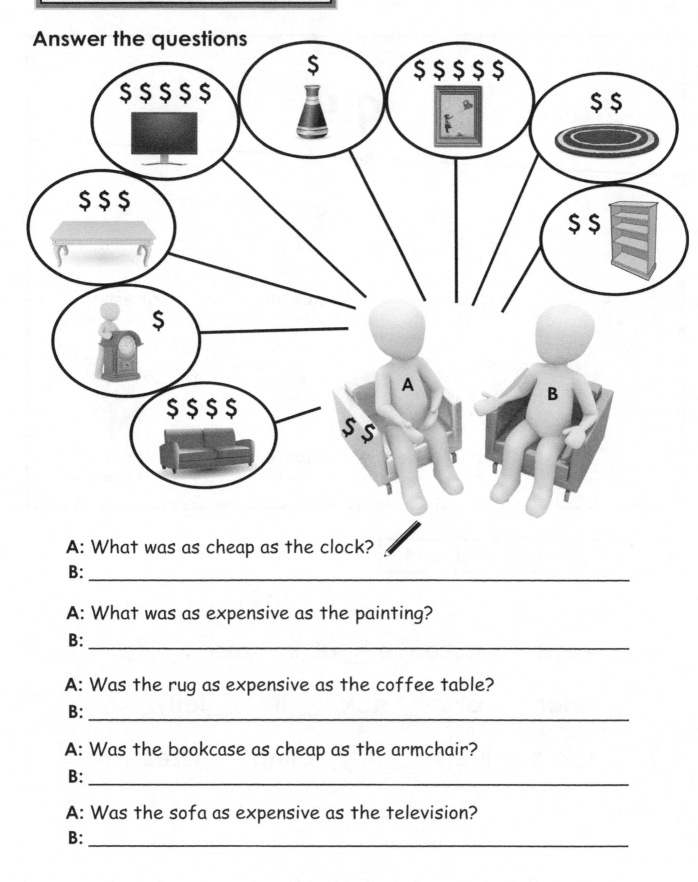

A: What was as cheap as the clock?

B: _____

A: What was as expensive as the painting?

B: _____

A: Was the rug as expensive as the coffee table?

B: _____

A: Was the bookcase as cheap as the armchair?

B: _____

A: Was the sofa as expensive as the television?

B: _____

навколо будинку

Part 1A: Learn the words

1. clean the **balcony**
   прибирати балкон
2. clean the **barbecue**
   чистити барбекю
3. fix the **fence**
   ремонтувати паркан
4. work in the **garage**
   працювати в гаражі
5. work in the **garden**
   працювати в саду

6. fix the **gate**
   ремонтувати ворота
7. fix the **mailbox**
   ремонтувати поштові скриньки
8. clean the **outdoor furniture**
   чистити вуличні меблі
9. clean the **pool**
   чистити басейн
10. work in the **yard**
    працювати на подвір'ї

 Practice speaking: "ремонтувати ворота " means "<u>fix the gate</u>"!

Part 1B: Write the words

Write the missing letters!   Write x 1   Write x 2

1. b__l__o__y   _____   _____
2. __a__b__c__e   _____   _____
3. f__n__e   _____   _____
4. __a__a__e   _____   _____
5. g__r__e__   _____   _____
6. __a__e   _____   _____
7. m__i__b__x   _____   _____
8. __utd__or f__rnit__re   _____   _____
9. p__o__   _____   _____
10. __a__d   _____   _____

How often do you <u>clean the pool</u>?

✓ I <u>rarely</u> clean the pool.

How often does she <u>work in the yard</u>?

✓ She <u>usually</u> works in the yard.

 Winner's Tip! Learn: never, rarely, seldom, sometimes, often, usually, always

Part 2B: Fill in the blanks

1. How _____ do _____ clean the _____?
   They seldom _____ the balcony.

2. _____ often _____ he work in the _____?
   _____ always _____ in _____ garden.

3. How _____ _____ she fix the _____?
   _____ sometimes _____ _____ fence.

4. _____ _____ do you _____ in the garage?
   _____ often work in _____ _____.

Do you <u>always</u> <u>fix the mailbox</u>?

✓ **Yes, I do. I** always fix the mailbox.

✗ **No, I don't. I <u>never</u>** fix the mailbox.

Does he <u>usually</u> <u>work in the garage</u>?

✓ **Yes, he does. He** usually works in the garage.

✗ **No, he doesn't. He <u>seldom</u>** works in the garage.

Winner's Tip! Remember: he / she / it: verb + s

Part 3B: Fill in the blanks

1. _____ you _____ fix the _____?
   Yes, I _____. I often _____ the gate.

2. _____ she usually _____ the pool?
   No, _____ _____. She never _____ the pool.

3. Does _____ always _____ the barbecue?
   Yes, he _____. He always _____ the _____.

4. _____ they _____ clean the outdoor _____?
   No, they _____. They rarely clean the _____ furniture.

Part 4A: Verb of the day

fix / fixes – fixed – fixing – fixed (ремонтувати)

I often need to <u>fix</u> things around the house.

Every month, he <u>fixes</u> his old, broken car.

They <u>fixed</u> the gate after the rainstorm.

He is <u>fixing</u> his dog's favorite toy right now.

She has <u>fixed</u> many of our problems.

Part 4B: Verb Practice

1. Each weekend, I _____ broken things in my kitchen.
2. On Saturdays, she _____ her old car in the garage.
3. Every week, he _____ the fence in his back yard.
4. Last month, they _____ the broken side window.
5. Last week, I _____ the sink in the bathroom.
6. Earlier today, we _____ the blender with his tools.
7. Right now, she is _____ the noisy coffee maker.
8. They are _____ it with the hammer right now.
9. She has never _____ her motorcycle before.
10. We have _____ that shelf many times already.

au / aw

/ɔ/

Other Words

au cause
faulty
launch

aw claw
crawl
flaw
law
prawn
raw

August
/ˈɔgəst/

auto
/ˈɔtoʊ/

sauce
/sɔs/

draw
/drɔ/

hawk
/hɔk/

straw
/strɔ/

1. Fl___ed ___to l___s c___se cr___ls.

2. ___gust r___ pr___n s___ce l___nch.

3. H___k cl___s dr___ f___lty str___s.

Match the words

mailbox garden

fence balcony pool

garage outdoor furniture

barbecue gate yard

work in the	clean the	fix the
1._____	2._____	3._____
_____	_____	_____
_____	_____	_____
	4._____	

Write the questions and answers

1.
never   rarely   seldom   sometimes   often   usually   always

A: How often do you _____?

B: _____

2.
never   rarely   seldom   sometimes   often   usually   always

A: Does he _____?

B: No, he doesn't. _____

3.
never   rarely   seldom   sometimes   often   usually   always

A: How often does she _____?

B: _____

4.
never   rarely   seldom   sometimes   often   usually   always

A: Do they _____?

B: Yes, they do. _____

Lesson 39 Daily life

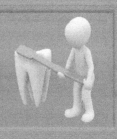

повсякденне життя

Part 1A: Learn the words

1. **brushed my teeth**
   почистили зуби
2. **cooked dinner**
   приготували обід
3. **done homework**
   зробили домашнє завдання
4. **eaten breakfast**
   поснідали
5. **gone shopping**
   пішли за покупками

6. **gone to school**
   пішли до школи
7. **gone to sleep**
   пішли спати
8. **taken a shower**
   прийняли душ
9. **taken out the trash**
   викинули сміття
10. **woken up**
   прокинулись

 Practice speaking: "прокинулись " means "<u>woken up</u>"!

Part 1B: Write the verbs

Write the missing letters!   Write x 1   Write x 2

1. b__u__h__d   _____   _____
2. __o__k__d   _____   _____
3. d__n__   _____   _____
4. __a__e__   _____   _____
5. g__n__   _____   _____
6. __o__e __o   _____   _____
7. g__n__ t__   _____   _____
8. __a__e__   _____   _____
9. t__k__n __u__   _____   _____
10. __o__e__ u__   _____   _____

<u>Yesterday</u>, when had you <u>eaten breakfast</u> by?

✓ **Yesterday, I had** eaten breakfast **by <u>half past nine</u>.**
✗ **Yesterday, I hadn't** eaten breakfast **by <u>half past eight</u>.**

<u>Last night</u>, when had he <u>gone to sleep</u> by?

✓ **Last night, he had** gone to sleep **by <u>a quarter to twelve</u>.**
✗ **Last night, he hadn't** gone to sleep **by <u>a half past ten</u>.**

 Winner's Tip! Learn: half past, a quarter past, a quarter to

Part 2B: Fill in the blanks

1. This morning, _____ had _____ woken up by?
_____, he had woken up _____ a quarter to six.

2. _____, when had _____ cooked dinner _____?
Yesterday, I _____ cooked dinner by _____ past five.

3. Last night, _____ had _____ gone shopping by?
_____, she hadn't _____ by _____.

4. _____, _____ had _____ done homework by?
Yesterday, he _____ done homework by half past nine.

Had you <u>taken out the trash</u> by <u>a quarter past four</u>?

✓ **Yes, I had. I had** taken out the trash **by** then.
✗ **No, I hadn't. I hadn't** taken out the trash **by** then.

Had she <u>gone shopping</u> by <u>half past two</u>?

✓ **Yes, she had. She had** gone shopping **by** then.
✗ **No, she hadn't. She hadn't** gone shopping **by** then.

 Winner's Tip! Use "then" for time in answer

1. _____ you brushed your teeth by a quarter to one?
   Yes, I _____. I had _____ by _____.

2. Had _____ taken a shower _____ half past eleven?
   No, he _____. He hadn't taken a shower _____ then.

3. _____ they _____ by a quarter to eight?
   Yes, _____ had. They _____ gone to school by then.

4. _____ _____ woken up by a quarter past nine?
   No, she _____. She _____ woken up by _____.

wake / wakes – woke – waking – woken (прокидатися)

Every day, I always <u>wake</u> up early.

Every morning, he <u>wakes</u> up at eight.

We <u>woke</u> up from a nap before dinner.

She is <u>waking</u> up very slowly today.

I have <u>woken</u> up late a lot recently.

Part 4B: Verb Practice

1. Every morning, I _____ up too late for breakfast.
2. On weekdays, she _____ up using her alarm clock.
3. Every weekend, he often _____ up early to exercise.
4. Yesterday, she _____ her friend with a phone call.
5. Last week, I _____ my dog when I got home late.
6. Last Saturday, the neighbor's party _____ me.
7. Right now, the baby is _____ up the entire house.
8. We are _____ up very early this morning.
9. He has never _____ up on time for classes before.
10. They have _____ up late every day this week.

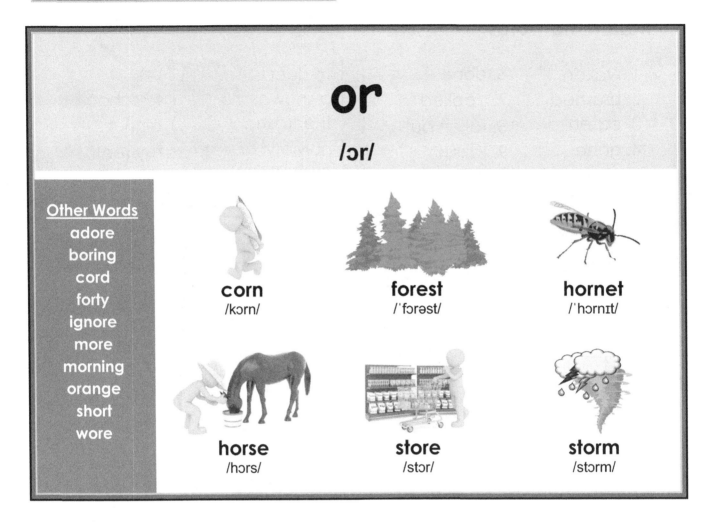

or
/ɔr/

Other Words
adore
boring
cord
forty
ignore
more
morning
orange
short
wore

corn
/kɔrn/

forest
/ˈfɔrəst/

hornet
/ˈhɔrnɪt/

horse
/hɔrs/

store
/stɔr/

storm
/stɔrm/

Part 5B: Write and read

1. B___ing h___ses ad___e ___ange c___n.

2. Ign___e sh___t f___est m___ning st___ms.

3. F___ty h___nets w___e m___e st___e c___ds.

Part 6: Fun review

Match the words

1. woken
2. brushed
3. eaten
4. gone
5. gone
6. done
7. cooked
8. taken out
9. taken
10. gone

☐ to sleep	1 up
☐ a shower	☐ to school
☐ the trash	☐ dinner
☐ homework	☐ my teeth
☐ shopping	☐ breakfast

7 am wake!

7:10 - 7:20 am teeth

7:30 - 8:00 am breakfast

8:15 am school

4:00 - 5:00 pm shopping

5:30 - 6:00 pm dinner

6:30 pm trash

6:45 - 8:30 pm homework

8:45 - 9:15 pm shower

10:30 pm sleep

Write the answers

1. Yesterday, when had he _____ by? [school]

_____

2. Had he _____ by half past nine? [shower]

_____

3. Last night, when had he _____ by? [homework]

_____

4. Had he _____ by a quarter to seven? [teeth]

_____

You: Yesterday, when had you _____ by? [sleep]

_____

Lesson 40 In the bedroom

в спальні

Part 1A: Learn the words

1. **bed**
   ліжко
2. **pillow**
   подушка
3. **mattress**
   матрац
4. **blanket**
   ковдра
5. **drawers**
   шухляди

6. **lamp**
   лампа
7. **alarm clock**
   будильник
8. **wardrobe**
   гардероб
9. **bed sheets**
   простирадло
10. **nightstand**
    тумбочка

 Practice speaking: "гардероб" is "_wardrobe_" in English!

Part 1B: Write the words

Write the missing letters!   Write x 1   Write x 2

1. __l_r__ __l_c__ _____ _____
2. __e__ _____ _____
3. b__d __h_e_s _____ _____
4. __l_n_e_ _____ _____
5. d_a_e_s _____ _____
6. __a_p _____ _____
7. m_t_r_s_ _____ _____
8. __i_h_s_a_d _____ _____
9. p_l_o__ _____ _____
10. __a_d_o_e _____ _____

249

Whose <u>alarm clock</u> is this?

✓ **This is hers. This is her** alarm clock.

✗ **This is not hers. This isn't her** alarm clock.

Whose <u>bed sheets</u> are these?

✓ **These are mine. These are my** bed sheets.

✗ **These are not mine. These aren't my** bed sheets.

 Winner's Tip! mine, yours, his, hers, its, ours, theirs

Part 2B: Fill in the blanks

1. Whose _____ is _____?
   That _____ _____. _____ is your blanket.

2. _____ pillows _____ these?
   _____ are not ours. These _____ _____ pillows.

3. Whose _____ _____ this?
   _____ is _____ his. _____ isn't his wardrobe.

4. _____ _____ _____ those?
   Those _____ theirs. _____ are _____ beds.

Is that his <u>lamp</u>?

✓ **Yes, it is. That** lamp **is his.**
✗ **No, it's not. That** lamp **isn't his.**

Are those our <u>drawers</u>?

✓ **Yes, they are. Those** drawers **are ours.**
✗ **No, they're not. Those** drawers **aren't ours.**

 Winner's Tip! Remember: this / that / these / those

Part 3B: Fill in the blanks

1. _____ these their _____?
   No, _____ not. _____ beds aren't _____.

2. _____ this my _____?
   No, _____ not. _____ mattress isn't _____.

3. Is _____ _____ _____?
   No, _____ not. That nightstand _____ his.

4. _____ those _____ blankets?
   Yes, _____ are. Those _____ _____ hers.

Part 4A: Verb of the day

change / changes – changed – changing – changed (міняти)

I usually <u>change</u> my pillow every summer.

Every day, he <u>changes</u> his T-shirt and pants.

They <u>changed</u> the mattress in the bedroom.

She is <u>changing</u> her job sometime next week.

We have <u>changed</u> our bathroom many times.

Part 4B: Verb Practice

1. Every week, I _____ the bed sheets in every room.
2. On Wednesdays, she _____ what she eats for lunch.
3. Every week, he _____ the music he listens to.
4. Yesterday, we _____ the blanket for a warmer one.
5. Last week, I _____ the time on my alarm clock.
6. Earlier today, she _____ the colors in her bedroom.
7. Right now, he is _____ his hat to a different color.
8. The weather is _____ a lot this season.
9. He has never _____ the old lamp in his bedroom.
10. They have _____ their jobs many times already.

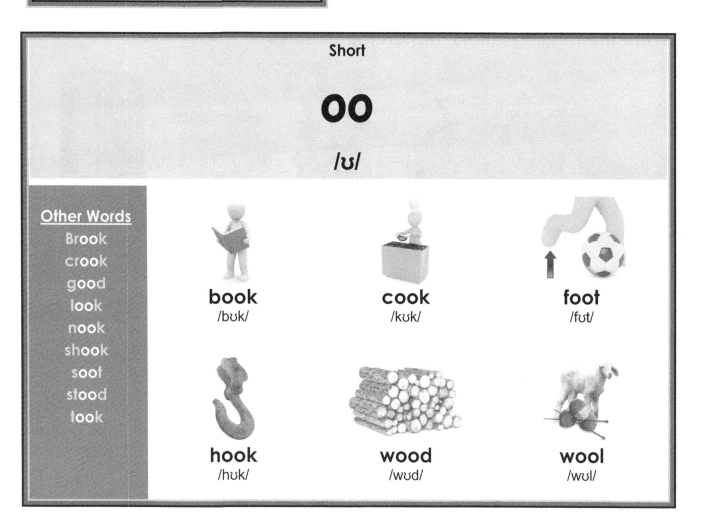

Short

oo

/ʊ/

Other Words
Brook
crook
good
look
nook
shook
soot
stood
took

book
/bʊk/

cook
/kʊk/

foot
/fʊt/

hook
/hʊk/

wood
/wʊd/

wool
/wʊl/

Part 5B: Write and read

1. Cr___ks sh___k w___den h___ks.

2. C___k's g___d f___t st___d l___king.

3. Br___k's w___l b___k n___k t___k s___t.

Part 6: Fun review

Write the missing letters, match the pictures

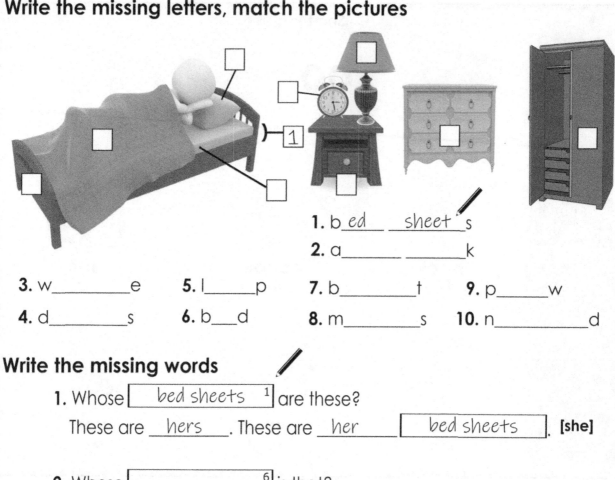

1. b_ed_ __sheet_'s
2. a_____ _____k
3. w_____e
4. d_____s
5. l____p
6. b__d
7. b_____t
8. m_____s
9. p____w
10. n_____d

Write the missing words

1. Whose [bed sheets ^{1}] are these?
   These are __hers__. These are __her__ [bed sheets]. **[she]**

2. Whose [^{6}] is that?
   That is _____. That is _____ [   ]. **[he]**

3. Are these _____ [^{4}]? **[you]**
   No, they're not. These [   ] aren't _____.

4. Is this _____ [^{7}]? **[they]**
   Yes, it is. This [   ] is _____.

5. Are those _____ [^{9}]? **[we]**
   Yes, they are. Those [   ] are _____.

Write the correct answer next to the letter "A"

A: ___ **1.** She likes to go _____ because it's _____.
a) camp / relax   **b)** camps / relaxes
c) camping / relaxing   **d)** camping / relax

A: ___ **2.** No, I _____. I think going fishing is _____.
a) won't / boredom   **b)** don't / bored
c) haven't / bored   **d)** don't / boring

A: ___ **3.** The painting _____ as _____ as the coffee table.
a) was / cheaper   **b)** is / more expensive
c) wasn't / cheap   **d)** has / cheap

A: ___ **4.** _____ the _____ as expensive as the vases?
a) Wasn't / clocks   **b)** Was / clocks
c) Were / clocks   **d)** Were / clock

A: ___ **5.** How often does he _____ the fence? He never _____ the fence.
a) fix / fixes   **b)** fixing / fixing
c) fixes / fixes   **d)** fixing / fixed

A: ___ **6.** _____ often _____ many things around the house.
a) He / fixing   **b)** We / fixes
c) They / has fixed   **d)** She / fixes

A: ___ **7.** Last night, he _____ brushed _____ teeth by half past nine.
a) hadn't / his   **b)** hasn't / his
c) haven't / my   **d)** wasn't / his

A: ___ **8.** No, I hadn't. I hadn't taken _____ by _____ to ten.
a) shower / quarter   **b)** a shower / quarter
c) a shower / a quarter   **d)** shower / a quarter

A: ___ **9.** Whose pillows are these? These are _____. These are _____ pillows.
a) hers / hers   **b)** her / her
c) her / hers   **d)** hers / her

A: ___ **10.** Are those _____ blankets? Yes, they are. Those blankets are _____.
a) your / your   **b)** her / her
c) my / yours   **d)** their / they

A: ___ **11.** _____ always _____ hiking in the mountains near his house.
a) He / enjoy   **b)** They / enjoy
c) We / enjoying   **d)** I / has enjoyed

A: ___ **12.** Right now, they _____ moving the television to the _____ room.
a) are / living   **b)** are / live
c) have / living   **d)** did / lived

A: ___ **13.** Does she usually clean the barbecue?
               Yes, she _____. She usually _____ the barbecue.
a) does / cleaning   **b)** cleans / cleans
c) has / cleaning   **d)** does / cleans

A: ___ **14.** He _____ up very early this morning. He usually _____ up late.
a) wake / wake   **b)** waking / wake
c) woke / wakes   **d)** had woken / woken

A: ___ **15.** In the wintertime, she _____ _____ blanket to a warmer one.
a) changes / her   **b)** changes / hers
c) change / hers   **d)** changing / her

A: ___ **16.** Was the bookcase as cheap as the coffee table?
               Yes, it was. It was _____ _____ the coffee table.
a) very / as cheap as   **b)** just / as cheap as
c) only / cheap as   **d)** just / as cheap at

A: ___ **17.** No, he _____. He rarely _____ the outdoor furniture.
a) hasn't / cleaning   **b)** didn't / had clean
c) doesn't / clean   **d)** doesn't / cleans

A: ___ **18.** Yesterday, _____ had _____ dinner by half past six.
a) he / cooks   **b)** she / cooking
c) I / cooked   **d)** we / cook

Answers on page 257

TEST ANSWERS

Test 1
1) c   2) a   3) b   4) a   5) d   6) c   7) d   8) b   9) d   10) a   11) c   12) c   13) b   14) d
15) c   16) a   17) b   18) d

Test 2
1) b   2) d   3) a   4) d   5) c   6) b   7) c   8) c   9) a   10) b   11) d   12) d   13) c   14) a
15) d   16) b   17) c   18) a

Test 3
1) d   2) b   3) c   4) b   5) a   6) d   7) a   8) a   9) c   10) d   11) a   12) b   13) a   14) c
15) c   16) d   17) b   18) b

Test 4
1) a   2) c   3) d   4) c   5) b   6) a   7) b   8) d   9) b   10) c   11) c   12) c   13) d   14) b
15) b   16) a   17) a   18) c

Test 5
1) d   2) c   3) d   4) a   5) b   6) b   7) c   8) d   9) c   10) a   11) a   12) d   13) b   14) a
15) b   16) b   17) a   18) d

Test 6
1) c   2) a   3) b   4) d   5) b   6) c   7) d   8) a   9) d   10) b   11) b   12) c   13) c   14) a
15) d   16) a   17) d   18) d

Test 7
1) b   2) c   3) d   4) b   5) d   6) a   7) b   8) b   9) c   10) d   11) a   12) b   13) c   14) d
15) c   16) a   17) b   18) c

Test 8
1) c   2) d   3) c   4) c   5) a   6) d   7) a   8) c   9) d   10) c   11) b   12) a   13) d   14) c
15) a   16) b   17) d   18) c

Other Great English Books for <u>Winners</u>!

Winner's early English For Ukrainian Speakers
Handwriting Practice, Vocabulary & Fun Worksheets

- *Winner's early English* – WEE learners Series – For Ukrainian Speakers: **Book 1 – Lessons 1 – 5**
- *Winner's early English* – WEE learners Series – For Ukrainian Speakers: **Book 2 – Lessons 6 - 10**
- *Winner's early English* – WEE learners Series – For Ukrainian Speakers
    (2-in-1 Book Version: Book 1 + Book 2 - Lessons 1 - 10)

Winner's English - Basic Lessons For Ukrainian Speakers
Beginner English, Phonics & Interactive Worksheets

- *Winner's English* - Basic Lessons For Ukrainian Speakers - **Book 1: Lessons 1 - 20**
- *Winner's English* - Basic Lessons For Ukrainian Speakers - **Book 2: Lessons 21 - 40**
- *Winner's English* - Basic Lessons For Ukrainian Speakers - **2-in-1 Book Series:**
    Book 1 + Book 2 (Lessons 1 - 40)

Preston's English for Winners! Verbs & Sentences - Ukrainian Version
Intermediate English, Verbs & Sentences, Essential Grammar

- *Preston's English for Winner's!* Verbs & Sentences - Ukrainian Version
    Book 1: Lessons 1 - 20

- *Preston's English for Winner's!* Verbs & Sentences - Ukrainian Version
    Book 2: Lessons 21 – 40

- *Preston's English for Winner's!* Verbs & Sentences - Ukrainian Version
    2-in-1 Book Series: Book 1 + Book 2 (Lessons 1 - 40)

Made in the USA
Las Vegas, NV
28 December 2023